Palgrave Studies in Leadership and Followership

Series Editor
Payal Kumar
New Delhi, India

Leadership has traditionally been defined as a process whereby an individual exerts influence over a group of individuals to achieve a common goal. While earlier theories placed the leader at the centre of the model, only recently has the other actor in the picture, the 'follower', become a focus for significant research and exploration. Within this context, however, the follower is still largely seen as a recipient of the leader's influence and power, who is subservient and passive, rather than as an organisational agent in his own right.

Palgrave Studies in Leadership and Followership aims to bring the follower-centric leadership approach to the fore. It is based on the premise that followers are largely proactive sense-makers who react in different ways to leadership and to change management. Adding value to leadership theory as well as organisational behaviour literature, this series situates leadership in the eye of the beholder, exploring how followers make sense of leaders and leadership, and what impact this has on their own identity, work relationships, the leader and the firm.

More information about this series at
http://www.palgrave.com/gp/series/15637

Shruti Vidyasagar · Poornima Hatti
Editors

Leadership and Role Modelling

Understanding Workplace Dynamics

palgrave
macmillan

Editors
Shruti Vidyasagar
Bengaluru, India

Poornima Hatti
Bengaluru, India

Palgrave Studies in Leadership and Followership
ISBN 978-3-030-09864-3 ISBN 978-3-319-69056-8 (eBook)
https://doi.org/10.1007/978-3-319-69056-8

Cover illustration: Jerome Murray - CC/Alamy Stock Photo

Printed on acid-free paper

This Palgrave Macmillan imprint is published by Springer Nature
The registered company is Springer International Publishing AG
The registered company address is: Gewerbestrasse 11, 6330 Cham, Switzerland

For my parents, Suma and Sagar. You made me who I am.
—Shruti Vidyasagar

To Siddhartha. You are my North Star.
—Poornima Hatti

Series Note

Leadership has been defined as a process that involves exerting influence on followers (Yukl, 2012). It is also said to consist of power dynamics in which leaders are bestowed authority and legitimate power by the organisation, largely because of their technical, human, and conceptual skills (Katz, 1955).

Earlier theories of leadership such as trait theory, or charismatic theory, placed the leader at the centre of the model. Followers were seen as recipients of a leader's influence and power, rather than as organisational agents in their own right, akin to devotees revering the leader as a God-like figure (Gabriel, 1997). From the role-based perspective of a follower in a hierarchical setting, even the word 'follower' implies that the agent is subservient and passive (Katz & Kahn, 1978).

More recently the 'other' actor in the picture, namely the follower, has become the focus of significant scholarly work (Baker, 2007; Bligh, 2011), including the follower's perception of the leader (Antonakis, House, & Simonton, 2017; Gottfredson & Aguinis, 2016). 'It is now widely accepted that leadership cannot be fully understood without considering the role of followers in the leadership process', (Uhl-Bien, Riggio, Lowe, & Carsten, 2014, p. 88).

Based on the assumption that the identities of both leaders and followers are socially constructed, interlinked and can transform each other (Meindl, 1995), this series intends to bring to the fore the follower as a largely proactive sensemaker who reacts to and shapes both leadership and organisational change. This merits deeper study, because the multi–faceted and ever changing follower identity is possibly more complex than was once thought (Collinson, 2006).

Gaining deeper insight into followers' identity, sensemaking, and co-construction of leadership is essential for the advancement of leadership knowledge (Brown, 2012) for several reasons:

- Followership determines how leaders are perceived (Carsten, Uhl-Bien, West, Patera, & McGregor, 2010).
- Followership identity predicts how a follower will follow, which affects both individual and organisational outcomes (Dasborough, Ashkanasy, Tee, & Herman, 2009).
- Followership predicts how a follower will lead (Koonce, 2013).

***

This book series follows seven different perspectives of key components in the follower–leader dynamic. Each volume consists of empirical and conceptual chapters on leadership and followership, interspersed with a few chapters by practitioners in the first person narrative style.

Each volume editor has chosen a specific aspect to explore in order to expand the full range of understanding of how followers shape leadership dynamics, largely from two levels of analysis:

1. Follower identity and behaviour at a micro level
2. Follower relationship with the leader at the dyadic level

What distinguishes this series from books in this domain is the distinct international appeal: The volume editors themselves span five countries (America, France, Australia, Canada, and India), and the research contributions are from scholars from all over the world. In fact, many of the volumes—such as on Authentic Leadership and Followership; The Dynamics of Role Modelling in the Workplace and Inclusive Leadership—Negotiating Gendered Spaces—explore this topic specifically from international and diversity perspectives. This series also has a strong interdisciplinary appeal, with the volumes drawing on perspectives spanning gender studies, philosophy, and neuroscience.

I have had the privilege of working with some fine scholars, who have worked diligently over the last few years to produce volumes, some of which are described below:

1. ***Servant Leadership and Followership: Examining the Impact on Workplace Behaviour*** 978-3-319-59365-4
   Editor: Crystal Davis
   Providing a deeper understanding of servant leadership and followership theory, this volume contributes to the literature on servant leadership and selfless service through the lens of the servant as follower. The collection brings together both empirical and conceptual research from around the globe that showcases servant leadership from the viewpoint of the follower.
2. ***Distributed Leadership: The Dynamics of Balancing Leadership with Followership*** 978-3-319-59580-1
   Editor: Neha Chatwani
   Challenging the current definitions of leadership by exploring more inclusive and holistic paradigms, this volume contributes towards the current discourse on distributed leadership by examining this as an inclusive form of leader–follower engagement. Qualitative and quantitative studies showcase the dynamics of followership in distributive leadership, covering several themes such as collective decision-making, leadership identity, roles, and demographic composition of groups in a variety of settings and human development processes.
3. ***Inclusive Leadership: Negotiating Gendered Spaces*** 978-3-319-60665-1
   Editors: Sujana Adapa and Alison Sheridan
   Questioning traditional perceptions of a leader as white and male, this volume presents leadership from a gender equity lens, and includes topics such as feminine leadership, leadership legitimacy and co-creating creativity between leaders and followers. With contributions from scholars in Australia, India, and the United Kingdom, this volume also touches on diversity within these countries, for example, Chinese migrants in Australia and Indian women accountants in Australia.

4. ***Authentic Leadership and Followership: International Perspectives***
   978-3-319-65306-8
   Editor: Dorianne Cotter-Lockard
   Authentic leadership, albeit controversial, is a well-accepted form of leadership. Given that the characteristics of authentic leadership and followership are largely context–specific, this volume explores leader–follower dynamics in different cultural contexts. This volume is divided into two broad themes: Global perspectives, including chapters from the Middle East, Mexico, and South Africa, and Conceptual perspectives, including chapters ranging from early career relationships to an existential perspective. The foreword to this volume has been written by Prof. William L. Gardner, a foremost expert on Authentic Leadership.
5. ***Leadership and Role Modelling: Understanding Workplace Dynamics***
   978-3-319-69055-1
   Editors: Shruti Vidyasagar and Poornima Hatti
   Presenting role modelling as an independent construct, separate from the other developmental relationships in the workplace, this volume is a deep exploration of role modelling as both a concept and as a dynamic process which impacts career development and outcomes. The chapters, consisting of literature reviews and research studies, reflect both academic and practitioner perspectives from across the globe. This volume also has sections on gender diversity and regional diversity (India).

To conclude, this series situates leadership in the eye of the beholder, exploring how followers make sense of leaders and leadership, and the impact this has on follower identity, work relationships, the leader, and the firm. 'Leadership is really not about leaders themselves. It's about a collective practice among people who work together—accomplishing the choices we make together in our mutual work', Raelin (2015, p. 96).

Payal Kumar
payalk1@gmail.com

References

Antonakis, J., House, R. J., & Simonton, D. K. (2017). Can super smart leaders suffer from too much of a good thing? The curvilinear effect of intelligence on perceived leadership behavior. *Journal of Applied Psychology, 102* (7), 1003–1021.

Baker, S. D. (2007). Followership: The theoretical foundation of a contemporary construct. *Journal of Leadership & Organizational Studies, 14*(1), 50–60.

Bligh, M. C. (2011). Followership and follower-centered approaches. In A. Bryman (Ed.), *The SAGE handbook of leadership* (pp. 425–436). London: SAGE.

Brown, D. J. (2012). In the mind of follower: Followercentric approaches to leadership. In D. V. Day & J. Antonakis (Eds.), *The nature of leadership* (331–362). Thousand Oaks, CA: SAGE.

Carsten, M. K., Uhl-Bien, M., West, B. J., Patera, J. L., & McGregor, R. (2010). Exploring social constructions of followership: A qualitative study. *The Leadership Quarterly, 21*(3), 543–562.

Collinson, D. (2006). Rethinking followership: A post-structuralist analysis of follower identities. *The Leadership Quarterly, 17*(2), 179–189.

Dasborough, M. T., Ashkanasy, N. M., Tee, E. Y., & Herman, H. M. (2009). What goes around comes around: How meso-level negative emotional contagion can ultimately determine organizational attitudes toward leaders. *The Leadership Quarterly, 20*(4), 571–585.

Gabriel, Y. (1997). Meeting god: When organizational members come face to face with the supreme leader. *Human Relations, 50*(4), 315–342.

Gottfredson, R. K., & Aguinus, H. (2016). Leadership behaviours and followership performance: Deductive and inductive examination of theoretical rationales and underlying mechanisms. *Journal of Organizational Behaviour.*

Katz, D., & Kahn, R. L. (1978). *The social psychology of organizations* (Vol. 2). New York: Wiley.

Katz, R. L. (1955). Skills of an effective administrator. *Harvard Business, 33*(1), 33–42.

Koonce, R. (2013). Partial least squares analysis as a modeling tool for assessing motivational leadership practices. In *International Annual Conference Proceedings of the American Society for Engineering Management, 2013 International Annual Conference.* Minneapolis, Minnesota.

Meindl, J. R. (1995). The romance of leadership as a follower-centric theory: A social constructionist approach. *The Leadership Quarterly, 6*(3), 329–341.

Raelin, J. A. (2015). Rethinking leadership. *MIT Sloan Management Review, 56*(4), 95–96.

Uhl-Bien, M., Riggio, R. E., Lowe, K. B., & Carsten, M. K. (2014). Followership theory: A review and research agenda. *The Leadership Quarterly, 25*(1), 83–104.

Yukl, G. (2012). Effective leadership behavior: What we know and what questions need more attention. *The Academy of Management Perspectives, 26*(4), 66–85.

Foreword

Role Models in the Workplace: Who Are They and What Can They Do?

Role modelling enables one to be an example who can inspire, motivate, and influence others. Merton (1957) first coined the term 'role models' to denote individuals who serve as examples of behaviours desired in specific roles (for example, a surgeon). Lockwood (2006, p. 36) notes: 'Role models are individuals who provide an example of the kind of success that one may achieve, and often also provide a template of the behaviours that are needed to achieve such success.'

Although the term 'role modelling' has been widely used in a variety of settings, its wide usage has not led to clarity about its meaning; instead, multiple perspectives exist about what constitutes role modelling. The purpose of this brief introduction to 'role modelling' is not to refute any of these perspectives; instead, my intention is to build awareness about the different perceptions to encourage a comprehensive understanding about who role models are in the workplace and what they can do.

While the central notion of 'role modelling' is that of being an example, different perspectives are prevalent about whether role modelling is only about exemplifying desired behaviours, or if it is also about inspiring possible identities in the workplace (Gauntlett, 2002; McIntyre, Paulson, Taylor, Morin, & Lord, 2011; Morgenroth, Ryan, & Peters, 2015). Morgenroth et al. (2015) proffer a broader definition of role modelling, delineating how role models can act as behavioural models through increasing one's self-efficacy, as representations of possible selves or identities through challenging self-stereotyping and changing perceptions of external barriers, and as sources of inspirations through changing one's values via personal identification and internalisation. Moreover, while some scholars do not consider interaction to be necessary for role modelling and provide instances of distant role models whose images are sufficient to inspire others to emulate them (Cotton, Shen, & Livne-Tarandach, 2011; Gibson, 2004), some believe that interaction is key to successfully emulating role models (Cheryan, Drury, & Vichayapai, 2013; Filstad, 2004). Role modelling is often denoted as a significant component of developmental relationships, specifically a function of workplace mentors (Ragins & McFarlin, 1990; Scandura & Ragins, 1993). It is typical to expect mentees or protégés to model their mentors' behaviours at work and to expect mentors to exemplify appropriate workplace norms. Thus, if one were to conceptualise 'role modelling' within the context of mentoring relationships, it does make sense to think of role models as someone who can be accessed and interacted with to clarify observable behaviours. This interaction then enables mentees to go beyond blindly observing and imitating mentors and adds a cognitive component of analysis and reflection to the behaviourist theory of social learning informing role modelling (Bandura, 1977a, b).

However, this conceptualisation does not discount the possibility that distant role models can be highly influential in individuals' lives. For instance, Cotton et al. (2011) found that members of National Baseball Hall of Fame attributed their career success to other players whom they emulated and respected as role models, but never met. Thus, even though leaders in top management may not have opportunities to interact with junior employees, they can be perceived as role models.

Furthermore, the notion of an absolute or total role model (that is, considering one individual to be the perfect role model who can be emulated) has also been challenged by scholars who claim that the workplace provides opportunities for learning from multiple individuals and hence, it is common for employees to have multiple contingent role models (Filstad, 2004; Gibson, 2004). Thus, one can choose to selectively emulate certain attributes and behaviours of multiple individuals and in doing so can exercise their judgement in determining how those multiple individuals can be considered role models in regards to specific skills and behaviours. This notion is comparable to the growing preference for developmental network with multiple mentors (Higgins & Kram, 2001) instead of the traditional focus on single mentoring relationships where one mentor had to bear the burden of meeting all developmental needs of the mentee. Instead, mentees are encouraged now to draw from the expertise of multiple mentors or developers and similarly, employees in the workplace can learn from observing and emulating multiple role models.

Whether it is a single role model or multiple role models, it is important to mention that unless the role model is perceived as relatable in a way that one can consider themselves attaining the goals achieved or pursued by the role model, it is unlikely that they will be emulated. Morgenroth et al. (2015, p. 472) explain this through the construct of attainability: 'A role model's attainability refers to the degree to which a role aspirant can see him or herself being like the role model in the future—the answer to the question "can I be like this person?"' Careful consideration of this construct urges us to rethink how role modelling can be effective to minority groups in workplaces. Often, organisations expect that if they have some exemplars of achievers from minority groups (for example, women, under-represented ethnicities, and cultures, etc.), those achievers should be able to inspire others to emulate them or to be inspired by them. However, if others do not consider those achievers as relatable or if they perceive the life conditions and successes experienced by those achievers as too difficult to pursue, then those achievers are less likely to be effective role models.

Of course, this perception of attainability is contingent on one's self-efficacy in terms of whether one thinks that they can emulate the achievers (Bandura, 1977a). But, this caution does imply that organisations need to do much more than having representation of minorities in leadership if they want to use role modelling as a developmental tool to encourage diverse employees to grow and prosper in workplaces. Organisations need to invest in understanding the complexity of the role-modelling phenomenon and prepare their employees to look out for role models whom they can emulate for developing both their skills and professional identities. At the same time, organisations need to encourage leaders in top and middle management to exhibit behaviours that can inspire employees to not only learn new skills, but also to aspire for achieving goals that may seem unattainable to many.

Given the potential of role modelling as a workplace developmental tool and the lack of comprehensive understanding of this phenomenon, this volume edited by Shruti Vidyasagar and Poornima Hatti on *Leadership and Role Modelling: Understanding Workplace Dynamics* is timely. The most notable contribution of this book is its dual focus on theory and practice. Often, scholarly publications tend to emphasise theory without giving due attention to application of theories and such efforts fall short of truly guiding practice. This book dedicates one section to highlighting theoretical underpinnings of the role-modelling concept and substantiates those underpinnings through practice-based case studies. Moreover, there is one more section entirely dedicated to practitioner perspectives on workplace role modelling in varied industries (legal practice, medicine, research, and academia, and business) in India. Most importantly, there is another section in this book that discusses the utility of role modelling as a developmental tool for women. As professional development and advancement of women are still faced with myriad challenges in workplaces, a guide on how to effectively use role modelling as a developmental tool for women is highly warranted.

Philadelphia, USA

Rajashi Ghosh
Associate Professor
Ph.D. Programme Director
School of Education Drexel University
rajashi.ghosh@drexel.edu

References

Bandura, A. (1977a). Self-efficacy: Toward a unifying theory of behavioral change. *Psychological Review, 84*(2), 191–215.

Bandura, A. (1977b). *Social learning theory*. Englewood Cliffs, NJ: Prentice Hall.

Cheryan, S., Drury, B. J., & Vichayapai, M. (2013). Enduring influence of stereotypical computer science role models on women's academic aspirations. *Psychology of Women Quarterly, 37*(1), 72–79.

Cotton, R. D., Shen, Y., & Livne-Tarandach, R. (2011). On becoming extraordinary: The content and structure of the developmental networks of Major League Baseball Hall of Famers. *Academy of Management Journal, 54*(1), 15–46.

Filstad, C. (2004). How newcomers use role models in organizational socialization. *Journal of Workplace Learning, 16*(7), 396–409.

Gauntlett, D. (2002). *Media, gender, and identity*. London, UK: Routledge.

Gibson, D. E. (2004). Role models in career development: New directions for theory and research. *Journal of Vocational Behavior, 65*(1), 134–156.

Higgins, M. C., & Kram, K. E. (2001). Reconceptualizing mentoring at work: A developmental network perspective. *Academy of Management Review, 26*(2), 264–288.

Lockwood, P. (2006). 'Someone like me can be successful': Do college students need same-gender role models? *Psychology of Women Quarterly, 30*(1), 36–46.

McIntyre, R. B., Paulson, R. M., Taylor, C. A., Morin, A. L., & Lord, C. G. (2011). Effects of role model deservingness on overcoming performance deficits induced by stereotype threat. *European Journal of Social Psychology, 41*(3), 301–311.

Merton, R. K. (1957). *Social theory and social structure*. New York, NY: Free Press.

Morgenroth, T., Ryan, M. K., & Peters, K. (2015). The motivational theory of role modeling: How role models influence role aspirants' goals. *Review of General Psychology, 19*(4), 465–483. https://doi.org/10.1037/gpr0000059.

Ragins, B. R., & McFarlin, D. B. (1990). Perceptions of mentor roles in cross-gender mentoring relationships. *Journal of Vocational Behavior, 37*(3), 321–339.

Scandura, T. A., & Ragins, B. R. (1993). The effects of sex and gender role orientation on mentorship in male-dominated occupations. *Journal of Vocational Behavior, 43*(3), 251–265.

Preface

Success in the workplace is attributable to many reasons—key among these is the ability to understand the ethos and culture of an organisation and build on it. This success is important for all stakeholders—leadership at the helm of the organisation, individuals within the organisation, as well as persons outside the organisation. The idea for this edited volume germinated when we were considering the impact of role models on fostering workplace cultures in the context of legal practice in India. We realised that often, role models not only drive young lawyers to excel in workplaces that are outside the direct sphere of influence of the role models themselves, but that they also do so by being almost entirely unaware of their effect on followers' careers.

While it is well-accepted that role models consciously (and unconsciously) help a person achieve success, what we wanted to understand better was, in the context of the workplace, where role models may be found, how a person finds them, how a person chooses one that works best for her, whether a person can have multiple role models, whether role models recognise that they are being followed, and so on. Acknowledging as we did that the workplace environment, especially a non-corporate structure, does not always provide a conscious opportunity or means to help a person grow, we were aware that she then chooses a role model on her own. If the idea of role modelling could be better understood in organisations, the impact of this kind of developmental relationship could be far greater—and more positive—on everyone in the workplace. This would be particularly relevant from the perspective of planning and transitioning leadership within organisations.

Initial conversations on these aspects clearly demonstrated to us that different cultural contexts and dynamics in the workplace, not to mention the very nature of the workplace itself, would determine the kind of role-modelling options available to a follower or protégé. Both of us, with significant exposure to workplaces surrounding the law and its practice, realised that even in legal practice, different jurisdictions and cultural aspects play out differently for followers, although leadership and success are goals that everyone aspires to at the beginning of their career. We also found that in many circumstances, and especially in fluid (unstructured or non-corporate) workplaces, there was no mapping of a follower, her role models, and the kinds of role models she may desire or need, prompting us to want to examine closely role modelling in the workplace from a follower's perspective. Formal and informal workplaces, structured and unstructured workplaces could all have different perspectives on what is needed to succeed. We felt there was a clear need to analyse and understand this premise.

Curiously, while there has been interesting and detailed scholarship on mentorship as a developmental relationship in the workplace (see, for example, Allen & Eby, 2007; Ragins & Kram, 2007), there is a dearth of studies on role modelling as a process, particularly from the follower's perspective. In this volume, therefore, we view role modelling as an independent construct, separate from other workplace developmental relationships, and explore whether it can, as a process, aid in career development and provide psycho-social support, akin to mentoring (Kram, 1985), in addition to shaping identity (Gibson, 2003, 2004), and providing the motivation and means to achieve goals (Lockwood & Kunda, 1997). We explore whether the dynamics of personal identification (Ashforth, Schinoff, & Rogers, 2016) result in choosing role models. We also examine the nuances between role modelling and mentorship, in different cultural and geographical backgrounds, while acknowledging that it is well-accepted that mentors should (if they are not already) be role models (Kram, 1985; Levinson, Darrow, Klein, Levinson, & McKee, 1978). Although there is some literature on the interplay between various mentoring programmes and role models in the context of shaping organisational cultures (Kane-Urrabazo, 2006), little is published on how role modelling and mentorship unfold differently, yet coexist and function effectively for followers and organisations as well as competent leaders, thus contributing to sustained career positioning and upward career mobility.

Role modelling in the Indian workplace is yet to be fully explored, even though some literature examines the dynamics of mentoring relationships (Ramaswami & Dreher, 2010) and considers how women professionals find limitations in enacting these relationships (Blake-Beard, 2015). In this volume, we consider special conditions of diversity in India, particularly how gender and the rural–urban divide determine not only the role-modelling process, but also role model identification, and how they may aid or pose challenges to reaping the benefits of role modelling. We also include practitioners' perspectives of role modelling in the workplace, which will give readers a hands-on understanding of how the process can work, both in general and in special workplace settings in India. Since most studies have so far emanated from the West, we focus on an Indian perspective, for insights from practitioners established and successful in their fields.

This volume is divided into three sections. In Section I, *Dynamics of Workplace Role Modelling*, we examine role modelling in the larger context of workplace developmental relationships. Through reviews of available literature, we attempt to understand the theoretical underpinnings of role modelling as a concept. We also explore how role modelling can be used as a developmental tool in the workplace, both from a follower's perspective and from that of the organisation.

In Chap. 1, titled 'A Followership Perspective on Role Modelling and Mentorship', Cassandra A. Ray and Michelle T. Violanti provide a conceptual foundation of role modelling and mentorship, elucidating co-cultural competence from a followership perspective. Given that followership characteristics and behaviours, such as co-cultural competence, self-regulation, and proactivity are widely desired attributes that are selected and perceived as meaningful through observation as individuals enact the cognitive processes of role modelling, Ray and Violanti explore how these associations influence individuals (identity, motivation to achieve goals, career,and psycho-social support) and workplace processes (socialisation, effectiveness, and training). They note that since role modelling has an individual-level propensity for developing either a new skill or a different style without interacting with the target, followership outcomes resulting from these attributes (social identity, influence, organisational climate, and power) offer valuable insight towards understanding how role modelling shapes identity and provides the motivation to achieve goals. Ray and Violanti expand on how effective followers engage in mentoring by interactively providing co-worker advice and support, and passing on specific skills knowledge during interactive processes.

In Chap. 2, titled 'Role Modelling and Its Impact on the Self-Development of Academics', through a comprehensive literature review, Julie Nyanjom explores the dynamics of role modelling in the context of higher education. Focusing on how role modelling can be used by academics to achieve pertinent self-development goals that institutions of higher learning expect from them, she discusses the intricate processes involved in how role modelling can positively influence the personal and professional development of academics, and examines theoretical perspectives of professional identity construction through role modelling. Nyanjom presents the view that academics will utilise role models for personal and professional development throughout their careers, and with this in mind, she examines the processes of role model selection and discusses the theoretical underpinnings guiding the achievement of self-developmental goals. Nyanjom concludes that role modelling can be applied as a tool to achieve personal and professional development for academics, while proposing practical recommendations to facilitate role-modelling interventions in the context of higher education and suggesting avenues for future research.

In Chap. 3, titled 'Role Modelling as an Alternative to Mentoring for Career Development Outcomes in Organisations', Tanjia M. Coleman presents a qualitative study based on interviews with diverse senior and middle-management leaders of corporations to discuss role modelling from a place of understanding, practice, and outcomes. Coleman views the outcomes of role modelling from two perspectives: sustained career positioning and upward career mobility, addressing questions such as (a) How is role modelling executed? (b) How will this shape organisations in the future? (c) How can those involved in role-modelling communicate the benefits and impact of role modelling in the workplace while differentiating it from mentoring, which can be a much more rigid and organised process? Analysing findings from the study, Coleman proposes a framework for role modelling, as a means for leaders to understand the impact, influence, and validity of role modelling.

In Section II, *Gender and Role Modelling*, we examine whether gender influences the dynamics of workplace role modelling. Using quantitative and qualitative studies, we consider the impact of gender on young adults studying in an American university and educated women from rural India in identifying role models and the role-modelling process.

We begin with Chap. 4, titled 'Close and Distant Female Role Models in the Workplace' by Alexandra L. Lyman and Stacie F. Chappell, who report on an exploratory study of young adults' perceptions of female role models in the workplace. Noting that the disproportionate ratio of male-to-female leaders—a reality of modern organisations—translates into fewer females being available as role models, they suggest that female portrayals in the media may be important as distant role models. Beginning with a background discussion of the role model construct, Lyman and Chappell report on the perceptions of participants in their study—which included male and female young adults—on role models in the workplace, comparing between the participants' perspectives and discussing how their chosen role models inform their leadership practice. Lyman and Chappell conclude with a discussion of their findings and recommendations for future practice and research.

In Chap. 5, titled 'Complexities in the Role Model Identification Process for Educated Women from Rural India', Annu Mathew examines the challenges faced by women from villages in India in fulfilling their career dreams. Their upbringing, amidst constraints of established gender roles, culture, religion, and family background diminishes the opportunity to dream big, often leading to anxiety, lack of exposure, and inexperience in identifying role models during the early stages of their life, and the inability to network as their career progresses. Mathew presents three case studies of women aged 35–60 years, observing that the workplace ecosystem, a crucial element in any good role-modelling process, is a completely new environment to these women, in terms of culture, people, rules, regulations, and mannerisms, and conquering such a workplace, in the absence of close workplace role models, is extremely challenging. Mathew concludes that when workplaces look for 'big dreamers with fire in the belly', this group of aspirants has all the behaviours for success—including a determination to achieve—except close role models.

In Section III, *Practitioners' Perspectives*, through papers written by successful practitioners established in their fields (senior lawyer, medical doctor and researcher, economist and academic, entrepreneur, and professional coach), we review how role modelling plays out in reality, and in particular, in Indian workplaces.

In Chap. 6, titled 'Role Modelling as a Means of Transformative Growth', Kshitij Sharma, a professional coach and trainer, explores how role modelling can be a pathway for transforming oneself to achieve desired outcomes not only in the workplace, but also in life. Sharma emphasises that role modelling is a powerful tool that enhances a person's effectiveness and brings about desired change in a short timeframe, and demonstrates the power of role modelling through illustrations and anecdotes drawn from his own work, while discussing powerful concepts such as the desire to learn and finding the right role model. Sharma also explains how role modelling can and does work, especially at the unconscious level, from the perspective of neuro-linguistic programming (NLP).

In Chap. 7, titled 'Fostering Vision, Culture, and Accountability in Young Organisations Through Role Modelling', Timothy Franklyn notes that there exist unique cultural and organisational challenges that present in an early-stage organisation (or a start-up environment). He discusses three different approaches to role modelling that founders can use to overcome challenges and achieve the objectives of the organisation: role modelling of vision, culture, and accountability. Drawing on available research in the areas of role modelling and entrepreneurship as well as the experience of managing young organisations by four entrepreneurs in their mid-thirties from Bengaluru (including himself, having founded a journalism school as an industry outsider), Franklyn discusses possible approaches to role modelling that can be effective in achieving the business and societal goals of young, emerging organisations. He concludes that founders, as role models, must be responsible to ensure that their actions reflect good values, which translate into the identity and culture of their organisations.

Chapter 8, titled 'Being and Following Role Models', is a combination of three narratives, based on authors' personal experiences with role modelling and mentoring in the fields of legal practice and advocacy, academia and administration, and medical practice and research. Each author, a leading practitioner in his chosen field, draws on his experiences from working in India and overseas, to write about being both a follower and a role model in the workplace. Remarkably, each of them concludes that modesty, humility, and self-reflection are essential hallmarks of being a role model.

In 'Finding Role Models Inside and Outside the Legal Profession', Raju Ramachandran, a senior advocate in the Supreme Court of India, writes about his personal experiences with role modelling during his legal career of more than 40 years. Ramachandran acknowledges that he has looked for, and found, role models outside the legal profession, while elaborating on what attracted him to his role models. In addition, he points out how, even after several decades of practice, he still looks for guidance from role models—on how to retire from the profession gracefully!

In 'The Personae of Role Models in Medicine and Research', T. S. Sridhar, a physician-scientist, highlights how medicine, as a practice and profession, lends itself to role modelling for effective teaching by preserving the core of the apprenticeship model. He cites role modelling as the most impactful method for conveying abilities beyond medical and clinical skills, such as observation and compassion. Sridhar mentions being introduced to mentoring as a conscious activity when he began his career in experimental biological research, recognising it as a time-intensive and challenging activity. He declares that being a role model is no less challenging, especially in imparting the ethical dimensions of research and practice, and concludes that only by holding oneself to the highest ideals can a person hope to be a responsible role model.

In 'Role Modelling as an Exercise in Self-Reflection', Sudarshan Iyengar, a lifelong Gandhian and former vice chancellor of Gujarat Vidyapith, the university founded by Mahatma Gandhi, discusses how Gandhi has remained relevant as a role model throughout Iyengar's career. He explains that Gandhi's principles of self-reflection, self-examination, and self-correction have guided and inspired him to be a better man and better professional, by looking inward. Iyengar also chronicles briefly the people and their work, both of which have inspired him in various workplaces during his varied career as a teacher, researcher, academic, and administrator.

We hope that this vibrant and diverse collection of chapters will advance thinking on role modelling in various contexts and in workplaces that are of a myriad hue, and ultimately, make workplaces more accessible and leadership more achievable for all.

We are immensely grateful to Dr. Payal Kumar for giving us an opportunity to contribute to this excellent series on Palgrave Studies in Leadership and Followership. This volume owes much to her prompt and sure guidance—she answered every query we have had readily and enthusiastically! Our sincere thanks to Dr. Rajashi Ghosh for writing the Foreword, giving the readers an insightful overview of the literature surrounding role modelling and putting this volume in perspective. We also greatly appreciate Dr. Aarti Ramaswami's kindness in writing an endorsement of the volume.

We want to acknowledge our respective spouses, whose help and cooperation were crucial in allowing us the time, attention, and energy needed to work on and complete this volume. Thank you!

We dedicate this volume to our respective parents, whose steadfast support and encouragement has helped us grow, dream, achieve, and aspire.

Bengaluru, India

Shruti Vidyasagar
Poornima Hatti

References

Allen, T. D., & Eby, L. T. (Eds). (2007). *The Blackwell handbook of mentoring: A multiple perspectives approach.* Malden, MA: Blackwell.

Ashforth, B. E., Schinoff, B. S., & Rogers, K. M. (2016). "I identify with her," "I identify with him": Unpacking the dynamics of personal identification in organizations. *Academy of Management Review, 41*(1), 28–60.

Blake-Beard, S. (2015). Confronting paradox: Exploring mentoring relationships as a catalyst for understanding the strength and resilience of professional Indian women. In P. Kumar (Ed.), *Unveiling women's leadership: Identity and meaning of leadership in India* (pp. 25–43). London: Palgrave Macmillan.

Gibson, D. E. (2003). Developing the professional self-concept: Role model construals in early, middle, and late career stages. *Organization Science, 14*(5), 591–610.

Gibson, D. E. (2004). Role models in career development: New directions for theory and research. *Journal of Vocational Behavior, 65*, 134–156.

Kane-Urrabazo, C. (2006). Management's role in shaping organizational culture. *Journal of Nursing Management, 14*, 188–194.

Kram, K. E. (1985). *Mentoring at work: Developmental relationships in organizational life.* Glenview, IL: Scott, Foresman.

Levinson, D. J., Darrow, C. N., Klein, E. B., Levinson, M. H., & McKee, B. (1978). *The seasons of a man's life.* New York: Knopf.

Lockwood, P., & Kunda, Z. (1997). Superstars and me: Predicting the impact of role models on the self. *Journal of Personality and Social Psychology, 73*(1), 91–103.

Ragins, B. R., & Kram, K. E. (Eds). (2007). *The handbook of mentoring at work: Theory, research, and practice.* Thousand Oaks, CA: SAGE.

Ramaswami, A., & Dreher, G. F. (2010). Dynamics of mentoring relationships in India: A qualitative, exploratory study. *Human Resource Management, 49*(3), 501–530.

Contents

Editors and Contributors

About the Editors

Shruti Vidyasagar is a lawyer and editor. She has pursued a varied legal practice in Bengaluru for several years, advising clients on several matters including foreign investment, employment, intellectual property, and corporate compliance. Shruti now advises several Indian and multinational companies on prevention of sexual harassment at the workplace, conducts training, and awareness sessions for personnel, and is an external member of committees set up to deal with complaints.

Shruti works as a freelance editor with *Oxford University Press, National Law University Delhi,* and *National Law School of India University*, editing books, reports, and journals. In addition, she consults with DAKSH Society, a Bengaluru-based organisation working on accountability in politics, governance, and the judiciary.

Her recent publications include:

- Vidyasagar, S., Narasappa, H., & Tirumalai, R. S. (Eds). (2017). *Approaches to justice in India: A report by DAKSH*. Bengaluru: DAKSH Society and EBC.
- Narasappa, H., & Vidyasagar, S. (Eds). (2016). *State of the Indian Judiciary: A report by DAKSH*. Bengaluru: DAKSH Society and EBC.
- Hatti, P., & Vidyasagar, S. (2015). Is sexual harassment at the workplace curtailing women's growth? In Payal Kumar (Ed.), *Unveiling Women's Leadership* (pp. 65–74). London: Palgrave Macmillan.

Shruti has a bachelor's degree in law (B.A.L., LL.B.) from Bangalore University and a master's degree in law (BCL) from the University of Oxford. She also has a postgraduate diploma in human rights law from the National Law School of India University, Bengaluru.

Poornima Hatti heads the dispute resolution team at Samvad Partners and is based out of Bangalore. Her primary area of practice is commercial and corporate dispute resolution as well as employment law. She has worked in India, United Kingdom, and in Singapore. She also sits as an arbitrator and mediator, and is a member of the LCIA–Young International Arbitration Group and the Australasian Forum of International Arbitration.

Poornima sits as an independent external member on committees to prevent sexual harassment at the workplace for various Indian and multinational companies. Poornima also teaches on invitation at various law schools in India. She enjoys reading stories to toddlers in her spare time.

Her recent publications include:

- Hatti, P., & Vidyasagar, S. (2015). Is sexual harassment at the workplace curtailing women's growth? In Payal Kumar (Ed.), *Unveiling Women's Leadership* (pp. 65–74). London: Palgrave Macmillan.
- Hatti, P., & Ravi, A. (2017). The costs of insolvency professionals—A challenge for trade creditors. *INSOL International*, Bangalore.

Poornima has a bachelor's degree in law from the National Law School of India University, Bengaluru, and was a Graduate Merit Scholar while she was reading for her LL.M. at the London School of Economics.

Contributors

Stacie F. Chappell is Assistant Professor at Western New England University with expertise in leadership effectiveness, spirituality, emotional intelligence, and ethics. Her doctoral thesis explored the relative contribution of IQ, emotional intelligence, and ego development to leadership effectiveness. Other current research interests include online teaching, compassion in organisations, and Giving Voice To Values. She teaches leadership, ethics, corporate social responsibility, and organisational behaviour. She is active in the AOM and serves as a member AOM's Management, Spirituality and Religion (MSR) executive, and a co-facilitator of the annual MSR retreat.

Prior to joining academia, Stacie worked as an organisational development consultant in Canada, Australia, Singapore, and Malaysia. She is a talented facilitator and has worked with individuals and teams at all levels of organisations in the public, private, and not-for-profit sectors. Her mission is to contribute to developing authenticity and leadership within and beyond organisations.

Tanjia M. Coleman is a human capital strategist with more than 15 years of experience working as a senior level human resources professional in Fortune 100 and large-scale companies including Kindercare Education, Microsoft, Starbucks, Sears, and Motorola. She is currently the Principal Consultant at Organisational Agility Associates (OOA), headquartered in Chicago, Illinois. At OAA, she focuses on optimising business efforts for organisations through organisation development initiatives such as strategic planning, executive team development, executive coaching, 360 feedback, evaluating, and redeveloping performance management processes and systems, and mentoring.

Tanjia earned her Ph.D. in Organisation Development from Benedictine University. In August 2016, she received the Best Paper Collaboration award from the Academy of Management, Management Consulting Division in Anaheim, California. Most recently, she completed research on strategic planning that has been published in the *Journal of Management Policy and Practice Volume.* She has completed over 50 research papers, presented as well as served as a reviewer and discussant at the Midwest Academy of Management, Southwest Academy of Management, Western Sciences Decision Institute, and the International Socio-Economic Institute of Firms and Organizations. Her work has been published in the *Recherches en Sciences de Gestion*, 2015.

Timothy Franklyn is an international corporate finance lawyer, having worked in New Delhi, Singapore, and Hong Kong in some of the world's most prestigious law firms. He regularly advised governments, corporations, and global investment banks on international capital markets transactions, including sovereign debt offerings, high-yield bond offerings, initial public offerings, and private placements. He has published several articles in the *Financial Times* as well as in the *Indian Business Law Journal.* He graduated from the London School of Economics with an LLM in International Business Laws. He currently serves as Chairman of National School of Journalism, Bangalore (NSoJ), which was established to produce journalists who care deeply about justice and democracy in India.

Timothy is a cancer survivor, who enjoys living life to the fullest by raising his three young children, fronting a rock band, studying biblical texts, dabbling in theatre, and playing cricket.

Sudarshan Iyengar is Chair Professor, Gandhian Philosophy, at the Indian Institute of Technology (IIT), Mumbai. He is the former Vice Chancellor of Gujarat Vidyapith, Ahmedabad (2005–2014), founded by Mahatma Gandhi. He is also a former director of the Centre for Social Studies, Surat (2004–2005) and the Gujarat Institute of Development Research, Ahmedabad (1999–2004). He is currently the Vice Chairperson of the High Level Dandi Memorial Committee and Member of the National Gandhi Heritage Sites Mission, set up by the Ministry of Culture, Government of India. He is also a member of the management boards of several voluntary organisations. He has been involved in the rehabilitation of tribal people displaced by the Narmada Dam Project in 1990s, and was active in the relief and rehabilitation of earthquake-affected people in Kachchh, Gujarat, in 2001.

Professor Iyengar has a Ph.D. in Economics, and the focus of his research includes Gandhian thoughts and practice, natural resource development and management, people and civil society institutions. He has published 65 research articles and 8 books, including his most recent work, *Gandhiji and Sanitation*, published by the Publication Division, Government of India, in 2016.

Alexandra L. Lyman holds a BA in Communication with a concentration in Media Theory and Production and an MS in Organizational Leadership from Western New England University. She is currently a senior copywriter in the University's division of Marketing and Enrollment Management, a contributor for *The Huffington Post*, and a media professional.

Annu Mathew is a research scholar in Human Resources at Xavier School of Business, XLRI, Jamshedpur, India. She is currently the Director for India Recruiting at Cerner Healthcare Solutions in Bengaluru, India. With 15 years of work experience, Annu has handled several roles (staffing, HR operations, HR business partner) and has been associated with several multinational corporations and start-ups. Her research interests include strategic human resource management, careers research, talent attraction, recruiting international human resource management, and workforce diversity. Annu has contributed a chapter on informal mentoring to an edited volume, which is currently in press.

Annu is a member of the Academy of Management and certified as a Global Professional in Human Resources (GPHR) from HR Certification Institute, as well as Behavioural Interview Master trainer from Development Dimension International (DDI).

Julie Nyanjom is a lecturer in Management at Edith Cowan University—South West Campus. Julie's research interests include organisational learning and development, hospitality and tourism practice, and education. Julie has been in the field of management training for the past 30 years and holds a Ph.D. in organisational behaviour, a master's degree in international business administration, and a B.Sc. in hospitality management.

Raju Ramachandran became a lawyer in 1976, after abandoning his initial plan of becoming a journalist. The Supreme Court of India designated him a senior advocate in 1996. He was Additional Solicitor General of India from 2002 to 2004. He has recently been *amicus curiae* in the Ajmal Kasab case, Nirbhaya case, and the Sabarimala Temple entry case. A selection of his articles written over three decades was published by Lexis Nexis in 2016 under the title *I've Been Around for Sometime*.

Cassandra A. Ray is a Ph.D. student in the College of Communication and Information at the University of Tennessee, Knoxville, USA. She received her M.S. degree in communication studies from the University of Tennessee, Knoxville. Her research interests are in the areas of followership and intercultural communication. Specifically, she studies how communicative characteristics and message production processes exhibit competence within leader–follower dyads as well as within culturally diverse relationships. Currently, she is a Graduate Teaching Associate and has taught undergraduate courses including on public speaking, survey of interpersonal communication, organisational communication, and research methods in communication lab.

Kshitij Sharma is an internationally certified executive coach (PCC), certified NLP Master Practitioner, and a leadership and management development trainer with over 20 years of global experience across diverse industries such as IT, BFSI, and ITES. He co-founded C2X, a training and coaching firm, in 2012. C2X has offices in 12 cities across India, with over 120 Maverick L&D Consultants associated with it. Prior to founding C2X, he worked in various senior positions in the training coaching and human resources departments of several multinational companies, including as the training lead of a global business at HSBC.

Kshitij has a postgraduate diploma in business administration from Symbiosis, Pune with a specialisation in Human Resources and completed his executive education from the Indian Institute of Management (IIM), Bengaluru.

T. S. Sridhar is a physician-scientist by training. He is currently Professor and Head of Molecular Medicine, St. John's Research Institute, Bengaluru, India. In his position, he heads a group of researchers working on the problem of heterogeneity in cancer, developing approaches to the molecular sub-stratification of cancer, so as to advise appropriate therapy for cancer patients. He trains doctoral students as part of his work.

Dr. Sridhar has been exposed to both the clinical and research worlds during his training in India and USA. In addition, he briefly flirted with the start-up world in the early noughties and was fortunate to have both companies acquired.

Michelle T. Violanti is Associate Professor of Communication Studies at the University of Tennessee, Knoxville, USA. She focuses on communication theory and methods with special attention to how language choices and culture affect people's interpretations and responses to messages. Specifically, Dr. Violanti studies how leaders (both organisational and educational) use language to create unity and identification, and have an impact on their workers'/students' organisational experiences. She has published articles in *Communication Education*, *Human Communication Research*,*Journal of Applied Communication Research*, and chapters in organisational and non-profit case studies books. She is the co-author of *Dynamic Public Relations: The 24/7 PR Cycle*.

List of Figures

List of Tables

Section I

Dynamics of Workplace Role Modelling

1

A Followership Perspective on Role Modelling and Mentorship

Cassandra A. Ray and Michelle T. Violanti

Introduction

Historically, the attraction to leadership has captivated a tunnelled focus on leaders primarily, masking followership as negative, banal, boring, or leadership's shadow, at best. The major global and academic antecedents responsible for shaping the unsavoury connotations signifying followership portray it as incapable, ineffective, defective, ordinary, or weak (Carsten, Harms, & Uhl-Bien, 2014). Consequently, the importance of

Authorship order is alphabetical: both authors contributed equally.

C. A. Ray (✉) · M. T. Violanti
School of Communication Studies, University of Tennessee,
Knoxville, USA
e-mail: cmellon2@vols.utk.edu; cassiemellon8@gmail.com

M. T. Violanti
e-mail: violanti@utk.edu

S. Vidyasagar and P. Hatti (eds.), *Leadership and Role Modelling*,
Palgrave Studies in Leadership and Followership,
https://doi.org/10.1007/978-3-319-69056-8_1

global followership has been largely overlooked, especially with regard to role modelling and mentorship.

Globally, followership research is of critical importance within organisations where these individuals' experiences have been positioned as inferior to the dominating interest of leadership. Certainly, leaders are not solely responsible for influencing organisational members and processes; rather, workplace outcomes are determined by the collective efforts of every employee. Correspondingly, the rising influx of diversity within national and international areas commands attention to the increasing amount of intercultural interactions experienced by organisational leaders and followers alike (VanderPal & Ko, 2014). Regardless of hierarchical position, communication among employees is at the crux of workplace relationships; because communication requires people to interact with each other, enacting followership inevitably happens in the midst of, and because of, diversity.

Dixon (2008, p. 163) emphasises, 'The role of the follower is not only to learn but to learn to teach. Followers teach their peers, new followers, and, perhaps most important, the leader'. Organisations thrive because they have members who are capable of engaging in teaching and modelling behaviours at all levels in the organisational hierarchy. As such, individuals perform follower roles differently, 'not all followers want to be leaders', and some are content to engage in both leader and follower roles without advancing positions (Baker, Stites-Doe, Mathis, & Rosenbach, 2014, p. 82). Thus, the term follower here is used to indicate a person who is not in a managerial or supervisory position based upon job title; in this role, followers have the opportunity to engage in both role modelling (that is, informal teaching) and mentoring (that is, formal teaching) behaviours. The purpose of this chapter is to connect co-cultural competence to the followership role by explicating how those who are better equipped to communicate appropriately and effectively across roles and with others who are culturally diverse are deemed as both more co-culturally competent and more effective followers. More specifically, it lays out a research roadmap including propositions to be considered and hypotheses to be tested within a framework of followership co-cultural competence.

Followership

Based on a constructionist view, followership and leadership are separate, yet complementary constructs, both being socially constructed relational processes between individuals (Uhl-Bien, Riggio, Lowe, & Carsten, 2014). Constructionist views of followership acknowledge that the way in which individuals enact a follower role depends on their unique characteristics, perceptions regarding leader and follower role orientations, ability to switch roles (that is, leader–follower switching), relationship with the leader, psychosocial aspects (for example, identity), and the context shaping any given experience (Carsten et al., 2014; DeRue & Ashforth, 2010; Popper, 2014; Sy & McCoy, 2014). Recently, Carsten et al. (2014) have directed attention to infusing a role-based approach with the constructionist perspective of followership, as co-constructed processes between individuals determining interactants' role orientation. This perspective suggests followers enact follower roles while acknowledging that the individual characteristics of a follower will play into the process of co-constructing expectations concerning organisational duties as well as the behaviours chosen while enacting a particular role.

Interestingly, role orientations are mutually influenced by communication encounters driving the co-construction of followership to solidify the interactants' expectations regarding role orientation for a given relationship or situation (Howell & Mendez, 2008). To elucidate, the process of socially constructing a follower's role occurs when interactants: (a) convey their own beliefs regarding organisational responsibilities and behaviours associated with roles, (b) internalise these expectations communicated by the other, and (c) form a tailored role orientation within that specific relationship or a given situation (Carsten et al., 2014; Howell & Mendez, 2008). Subsequently, followers' behaviours reflect these relationally established role perceptions. Although follower behaviours reflect their role perceptions, the effectiveness of enacted behaviours relies largely on personal characteristics. Importantly, this process avoids restricting organisational members to a concrete role prescription based on hierarchical rank; rather, taking a relational approach to define followership accounts for factors influencing the outcome (that is, personal characteristics, relationship, organisational context), which guide the individuals who form workplace relationships. Therefore, followership illustrates the characteristics, behaviours, and processes one engages in while interacting with others, and as a result of the role prescriptions developed in relation to the leader, in an effort to meet personal and organisational objectives to produce desired outcomes (Carsten et al., 2014; Uhl-Bien et al., 2014). However, understanding what characteristics separate a follower from an effective follower as individuals enact the behaviours associated with these roles affords the opportunity to explore the nature and processes of followership within national and global workplaces relevant to role modelling and mentorship.

It is important to differentiate between an employee and a follower as well as the difference between a follower and an effective follower. Employees are organisational members who do not possess a leadership title or role as well as choose or are forced not to enact a followership role. For example, independent consultants who are part of multilevel marketing organisations, some computer programmers, and janitorial staff may all find themselves serving as organisational employees but not necessarily be followers. At baseline, 'subordination is a requirement of hierarchical position defined by power and status' where all employees are subordinates; however, employees choose whether to engage in a follower role (Hinrichs & Hinrichs, 2014, p. 92). This demarcates an employee from a follower.

An effective follower is an individual enacting a follower role 'who shares in an influence relationship among leaders and other followers' to produce desired outcomes (Adair, 2008, p. 139). When performing a follower role, there are three behavioural orientations manifesting followership roles, including: (a) an interactive orientation distinguished by behaviours serving to support and advocate the values and objectives of a leader, (b) an autonomous orientation reflecting follower tendencies to act more as independent agents from a leader, and (c) a shifting orientation, indicative of a collectivistic approach that followers demonstrate by enacting either a leadership or followership position depending on the particular role the group needs them to play (Howell

& Mendez, 2008). First, followers engage in an interactive orientation on a continuum of participative role characteristics ranging from passive to active to proactive behaviours (Epitropaki, Sy, Martin, Tram-Quon, & Topakas, 2013). To elucidate, Carsten, Uhl-Bien, West, Patera, and McGregor (2010) found subtle behavioural differences between the three roles encompassing the interactive orientation, where followers who enact: (a) a passive role emphasise adherence to leaders' orders, deference, loyalty, and advancing leaders' initiatives, (b) an active role demonstrate conditional voice (that is, offering feedback only when asked), obedience, and loyalty despite differing opinions, and (c) a proactive role take initiative, voice (that is, constructively conveying opinions that differ), and interacting in a collegial manner. Similarly, the independent and anti-authoritarian follower roles anchor opposite ends of the autonomous orientation spectrum. An independent role involves self-managing behaviours using one's own self-direction to accomplish tasks, whereas anti-authoritarian followers resist, avoid, disregard, or oppose a leader (Carsten et al., 2014; Howell & Mendez, 2008). Generally, independent, proactive followers are preferred to anti-authoritarian, passive followers in all cases except where the leader is performing poorly, unethically, or outside acceptable organisational norms.

Indeed, proactive behaviours provide a compelling means for determining effectiveness. Under the right circumstances, passive, active, or independent behaviours can also serve to demarcate follower effectiveness. In fact, research indicates both interactive (that is, passive, active, and proactive) and independent followers all include qualities of effective followers or developing follower effectiveness (Baker et al., 2014; Jaussi & Randel, 2014). Not surprisingly, anti-authoritarian behaviours tend to carry a negative connotation related to ideas of egregious behaviours and thus are generally considered ineffective. However, followers may find themselves in an unsavoury or unique situation where these behaviours can be effectively utilised (Baker et al., 2014). Above all, role behaviours do not necessarily guarantee that a follower has the ability or knowledge of how to utilise these behaviours appropriately to produce desired outcomes. Determining follower effectiveness without considering the influence of contextual factors, such as culture, is suspect at best. Thus, emphasising the importance of followers engaging in a shifting orientation and identifying the sources/personal characteristics that underscore the behaviours enacted within follower roles delineates a follower from an effective follower.

Co-culturally Competent Followership

Co-cultural competence concerns social functioning by emphasising the ability to interact effectively and appropriately with others who are culturally diverse. In an effort to enhance clarity, the term co-cultural competence was chosen over intercultural competence to indicate that subcultures and diversity exist locally, nationally, and internationally. Historically, communication competence has been depicted as a dyadic process functioning based upon both parties' motivations (that is, affect), knowledge (that is, cognition), and skills (that is, behaviours) within a specific episode (Spitzberg, 2000). Therefore, co-cultural communication competence is conceptualised as effective and appropriate interactions that accomplish the objectives within a given situation between two or more people who, as a result of culture, have different cognitive, affective, and behavioural orientations (Arasaratnam, 2014; Spitzberg & Changnon, 2009). Increasing diversity and globalisation spikes the occurrence of experiencing co-cultural interactions from occasionally to often daily.

Motivation, knowledge, and skills generally characterise one's co-cultural competence; however, everyone needs a baseline set of competencies to function in everyday interactions. Notably, 'no list fits all cultures, all contexts, all conditions'; however, lists that consider cognitive, affective, and behavioural capacities do provide adequate starting points regarding the assessment of characteristics for a specific case (Bennett, 2009). There is no magical list that automatically makes someone co-culturally competent in every situation; rather, baseline competencies, broad attributes of motivation, knowledge, and skills, afford an individual the opportunity to create shared meaning by voluntarily and deliberately adapting messages to match the context. For example, a follower and a leader may both have the same knowledge and skills; however, they may not make effective choices of when, where, and how to use that expertise or skill set. Co-culturally competent organisation members make the right decision for the situation; co-culturally incompetent organisation members make the situation match their communication choices without taking the others involved into consideration. Thus, co-culturally competent communicators have personal, dyadic, and organisational goals that align to create shared meaning and those who are co-culturally incompetent emphasise one goal to the detriment of the others.

To be a co-culturally competent follower, organisations seek members who possess the ability to interact both effectively and appropriately. Attributes of a co-culturally competent follower include: goal-directed self-regulation, flexibility/adaptability, and credibility.

Goal-Directed Self-Regulation

Goal-directed followers are perceived to be effective by others (Junker & van Dick, 2014; Korsgaard, Meglino, Lester, & Jeong, 2010). Organisational goals prescribed to followers are optimally achieved when an individual organises emotions and cognitions in a way that sparks motivation; the result is desired outcomes. Therefore, utilising self-regulation to adapt behaviours aimed towards goal achievement is imperative to effective followership. Self-regulation refers to 'the exercise of control over oneself, especially with regard to bringing the self into line with preferred standards encompassing any efforts to alter inner states (that is, cognitive or affective) or responses' (Carver & Scheier, 2004, p. 2). Goal-directed self-regulation includes adjusting individual behaviours towards goal achievement through the process of: (a) setting standards of behaviour that facilitate goal expectations, (b) detecting discrepancies, which occurs when a comparison between set standards and an individual's current state do not align, and (c) matching behaviours to the set standards (Carver & Scheier, 1981; Tsui & Ashford, 1994). Thus, co-culturally competent followers are both willing and able to set their own standards for achieving goals, compare their own behaviours to the standards of others both cognitively and affectively, and adopt behaviours or develop skills that allow them to reduce any discrepancies between their current behavioural state and the desired standard state.

Once goals activate the regulatory processes and illuminate the extent of self-motivation, followers must be willing to engage in communicative behaviours that successfully reduce discrepancies impeding goal attainment. Effective followers achieve goals efficiently through the process of recognising and utilising intrinsic motivations to complete tasks as well as actively participating with diverse co-workers in joint tasks. Therefore, goal-directed self-regulation illustrates self-motivation and willingness to engage, which are then utilised effectively towards individual and/or organisational goal achievement. Moreover, both affective and cognitive regulatory components serve to encourage effective follower behaviours vital to achieving a mutual understanding necessary for optimal goal attainment (Lockwood, Seara-Cardoso, & Viding, 2014). Overall, shared understanding of both the goals and how to achieve those goals also requires all parties involved to be capable and willing to engage in cognitive and behavioural flexibility.

Flexibility (Cognitive and Behavioural)

Research indicates effective followers adapt their followership style to meet the needs of a situation (Carsten et al., 2010). Communication adaptability is defined as the 'ability to change our interaction behaviours and goals to meet the specific needs of the situation' (Ting-Toomey, 2009, p. 103). Both cognitive and behavioural flexibility are key components of adaptability, governing follower appropriateness. Cognitive flexibility concerns the 'ability to shift frames of reference' characterised as being: 'open to new information, aware of more than one perspective', and mindful of divergent interpretations of messages and situations, whereas, behavioural flexibility refers to 'the ability to adapt and accommodate one's own behaviour to people from other groups' (Pusch, 2009, pp. 69–70). Those who are cognitively flexible understand that how they craft a message for someone from an accounting department is going to be different from how they craft a message on the same topic for someone from a marketing department because those two aspects of an organisation have different organisational cultures and see the bottom line/profit and loss very differently. Similarly, those who are behaviourally flexible choose to use the appropriate message for accounting when they interact with accountants and for marketing when they interact with those from marketing. Just because people have the ability to interact competently by crafting effective messages does not mean they always engage in the appropriate behaviour by utilising the message that is more likely to be effective.

A co-culturally competent follower's cognitive complexity (Delia, 1977; O'Keefe & Sypher, 1981) undergirds the mental foresight required to engage in cognitive and behavioural flexibility in a manner that exhibits appropriate forethought and action. For example, Dawidziuk, Boboryko-Hocazade, and Mazur (2012) reveal that individuals incorporate components of cognitive flexibility into work processes such that individuals who are high in cognitive flexibility view cultural differences positively, are able to make sound decisions, and deal with uncertain situations. Because uncertainty does not allow people to draw upon scripts that they have previously developed, they need to have the cognitive ability to draw conclusions about a new context without benefit of trial and error. Therefore, both forms of flexibility are needed to properly accomplish personal, relational, and collective organisational goals.

Credibility

Credibility allows a follower to utilise ethos, expert power, and interpersonal power to accomplish individual, dyadic, group, and organisational goals. Communication drives relational interactions and serves as a basis for forming or influencing individual judgements. The degree of influence followers have is based upon expert or interpersonal power stemming from their knowledge, character, and skills (Hinrichs & Hinrichs, 2014). Demonstrating co-cultural competence through effective and appropriate behaviours involves constructively influencing others with one's credibility. Reflecting the Aristotelian concept of ethos, source credibility, composed of expertise, character, and caring, has been defined as 'the attitude toward a source of communication held at a given time by a communicator' (McCroskey & Teven, 1999; McCroskey & Young, 1981, p. 24). First, expertise concerns perceptions of qualification, intelligence, knowledge, and authoritativeness, which are commonly associated with perceptions of competence (McCroskey & Teven, 1999). Different kinds of expertise, ranging from technical issues to mundane tasks, are needed when organisational members work together to achieve organisational goals (Stech, 2008). Co-culturally competent followers raise awareness of their own expertise as well as the expertise of others within diverse teams to influence teaching opportunities and collaboration, which encourages goal achievement through collective action.

Second, character (that is, dynamism) refers to perceptions of trust, honesty, and sagacity (Berlo, Lemert, & Mertz, 1969; McCroskey & Teven, 1999). The meaning of trust varies across cultures; however, all trust is a process of reducing uncertainty (Avolio & Reichard, 2008). Co-culturally competent followers reduce uncertainty to build trust by revealing characteristics of openness to different perceptions regarding methods of practice or ethics, while dually communicating messages honestly through repeated interaction to increase social identification and perceived interdependence (Avolio & Reichard, 2008). Moreover, trust, social identification, and reduced uncertainty fulfil the socio-psychological need for belonging (Popper, 2014). Thus, a follower's character stimulates a sense of shared identity with others and augments one's power to influence based on expertise and liking to help achieve individual and collective goals.

Third, caring refers to empathy, understanding, goodwill, and responsiveness (McCroskey & Teven, 1999). Influencing another individual's judgements through competent behaviours requires followers to express and respond to messages complementary to the mindset of the other to gain attention and support. As such, this involves understanding the perceptions of the other person, a core aspect of empathy. Importantly, mutual understanding between relational partners is an outcome of empathy that heightens shared identity, closeness, and cooperation (de Vignemont & Singer, 2006; Goldstein, Vezich, & Shapiro, 2014). Therefore, empathy is a skill affording followers the ability to tailor follower roles and behaviours with culturally different partners in a way that bolsters attempts to influence based on expert or interpersonal power aimed towards promoting cohesion and synergy that are often necessary for goal achievement within workplaces.

Followership Role Modelling

Distinguishing Between Mentoring and Role Modelling

Followers serve as both role models and mentors. There is more room for people to perceive similarities than differences between the two roles. This may be, in part, because mentoring is often viewed by organisations and their members as part of the formal processes and roles to and against which organisational members are assigned and evaluated. For example, there are no formal training programmes or handbooks on how to be an effective role model in individual organisations; however, mentors receive specific clear guidelines for engaging in their mentoring tasks as well as formal or informal training on how to further develop those mentoring skills. Because mentoring is often a formally assigned role, mentoring can be viewed as a one-way street with the mentor actively engaging in the process and the mentee being a passive recipient of the communication, information, and advice. Kram (1985) defined psychosocial (that is, helping the person handle the day-to-day aspects of organisational functioning) and career (that is, helping the person develop on a career trajectory to advance one's organisational position or be in a better position to change organisations) types of mentoring. In each of these cases, the more senior person would 'do' the mentoring work and the mentee would 'receive' the benefits of that work. While the mentor may benefit in this relationship, there are no guarantees.

Whereas, mentoring relationships tend to be more formal in nature, role-modelling behaviours, and the relationships that develop from them tend to be more informal in nature. For example, a mentor is likely to tell the protégé what the employee manual says about how to maintain safety on the warehouse floor and a role model is likely to enact the behaviours that she or he has developed for maintaining safety that may extend beyond what is available in an employee manual. For our purposes, role modelling and mentorship coexist and function effectively in the followership arena. Traditionally, research reveals followers benefit from role models and mentors (Ghosh, 2012; Gibson, 2003); however, individuals who excel within their sphere of interest can be seen as role models who are accomplishing both individual and organisational goals.

Followers' Co-cultural Competence and Role Modelling

Effective followers serve as role models because followership characteristics and role behaviours, such as co-cultural competence and proactivity, are widely desired attributes that are selected and perceived as meaningful through observation as individuals enact the cognitive processes of role modelling (Carsten et al., 2010). An individual's place of work is the most proximal context in which similarity comparisons can be made (Hogg & Terry, 2000); however, personal networks (for example, peers, colleagues, and acquaintances) extend beyond the organisational home. As such, effective followers are more available, which increases the frequency of interactions and opportunities for role modelling. Therefore, a follower's co-cultural competence and role behaviours are observable attributes ripe for selection.

A role model is a cognitive representation 'based on the attributes of people in social roles an individual perceives to be similar to him or herself to some extent and desires to increase perceived similarity by emulating those attributes' (Gibson, 2004, p. 136). However, role modelling is 'a cognitive process in which individuals actively observe, adapt, and reject attributes of multiple role models' (Gibson, 2004, p. 136) who are perceived to be similar. Role modelling reflects an intrapersonal process and individual-level propensity for either a new skill or a different style with or without interacting with the target. As such, it is a fundamental process of, personal development throughout the lifetime of one's career; however, the purpose of adapting or rejecting different role model attributes varies depending upon career stage (Gibson, 2003). Research reveals (Gibson, 2003) that the purpose of role model construal is determined by the current phase of one's career, where individuals in their: (a) early career stages pursue acquiring maximal information regarding a multitude of positive attributes to forge self-concept, (b) middle career stages select specific positive and negative attributes to sharpen/refine self-concept, and (c) late career stages aim to solidify self-concept by averting from negative role model attributes and gaining new skills through specific attributes of positive role models. Thus, individuals consistently seek role models using the process of role modelling to develop a self-concept that promotes competence (to be more effective, appropriate, skilled), career advancement, and job security throughout the career lifespan.

From a communication perspective, role modelling can also be viewed as interactive whereby the co-culturally competent follower and person seeking role modelling interact with each other. This type of communication provides socio-psychological and career support that differs from mentoring in two ways: (a) interactions are more informal based on perceived similarity and (b) interactions influence and shape multiple layers of an individual's identity. First, role modelling as an interactive process is based on the perceived similarities between individuals, rather than power or status differentials when the purpose of communication is to fulfil one's desire to learn or adapt an attribute demonstrated by another. Co-culturally competent followers' character, goodwill, and intelligence (that is, credibility) work in tandem to create a more informal communicative environment that establishes a sense of camaraderie and security when others interact with them as role models. This type of collegial informality influences how people communicate and define their personal and relational layers of identity (Hecht, 1993, 2015), such that individuals feel more free to express their opinions, convey how they define themselves either as unique human beings or by their relationship roles, or articulate how others see them. As such, interactants understand each other better and further their relationship, presenting an opportunity to extend socio-psychological support as well as broaden networks and resources to advance career support. Co-culturally competent followers can also engage in role modelling interactively through self-regulatory attributes.

Second, co-culturally competent followers model and communicate attributes such as goal-directed self-regulation and flexibility through effective behaviours while accomplishing tasks. During the interactive role-modelling process, the interplay between co-culturally competent followers' cognitive and behavioural flexibility reduces uncertainty and shapes the seeker's enactment layer of identity. Individuals observe, adapt, or reject attributes of role models as they encounter uncertainty while completing routine operations, prescribed tasks, and workplace processes such as socialisation and training. Followers use cognitive and behavioural flexibility to craft informative or instructional messages about attributes and tailor disclosing information to match the situation in a way that provides clarity and understanding, thus reducing seeker uncertainty. The transferred information is either adopted or rejected by the seekers, shaping their identity and influencing enacted behaviours that communicate identity as a function of performance. Furthermore, research suggests that effective followers can either promote or suppress the collective emotions of organisational members when there is heightened identification between group members and the effective follower (Tee, Paulsen, & Ashkanasy, 2013). Members who have a sense of shared identity also share a sense of communal orientation. As such, goals can be automatically activated within individuals who possess communal relationship orientations when they are either prescribed goals or when they observe goal pursuit as a social responsibility behaviour modelled by others (Fitzsimons & Bargh, 2004). Therefore, co-culturally competent followers are able to actively and interactively provide other organisational members, both peers and those in subordinate or superior positions, with concrete examples of how to behave or communicate to achieve individual and organisational goals.

Future Research

Because followership, co-cultural competence, and role modelling have not been examined in combination with each other, the following two propositions are proposed:

1. More co-culturally competent followers are perceived as more effective followers.
2. More co-culturally competent followers are perceived as more effective role models.

Working with these two propositions as a starting point, the following hypotheses are proposed as areas ripe for future study to better understand the relationships between and among the various aspects of effective followership, co-cultural competence, and role modelling.

Effective Followership

1A. There is a direct relationship between credibility and perceptions of effective followership.
1B. There is a direct relationship between self-regulation and perceptions of effective followership.
1C. There is a direct relationship between (a) cognitive and (b) behavioural adaptability and perceptions of effective followership.
1D. Credibility is the strongest predictor of effective followership followed by self-regulation and finally cognitive and behavioural adaptability.

Role Modelling

2A. There is a direct relationship between credibility and perceptions of effective role modelling.
2B. There is a direct relationship between self-regulation and perceptions of effective role modelling.
2C. There is a direct relationship between (a) cognitive and (b) behavioural adaptability and perceptions of effective role modelling.
2D. There is a direct relationship between effective followership and role modelling.
2E. Effective followership is the strongest predictor of effective role modelling followed by credibility, cognitive and behavioural adaptability, and finally self-regulation.

Assessing Role Modelling

An immediate first step for research studying followership co-cultural communication competence and role modelling is developing and validating instruments for assessing role-modelling selection and effectiveness. An instrument designed to assess role model selection should extend Gibson's (2004) framework comprised of two assessment dimensions, each containing two sub-scales, including: (a) the cognitive dimension stems from perceptions of similarity, measuring selection based on whether attributes are positive/negative and global/specific and (b) the structural dimension stems from aspects concerning proximity within organisational structures, measuring selection based on amount of interaction (that is, close/distant) and hierarchical position (that is, up/across-down). Additionally, exploratory research conducted by Gibson (2003) found that individuals engage in role modelling to advance their professional identity in different ways depending on career stage. An instrument designed to determine role model effectiveness should expand on this finding to measure the degree to which role modelling fulfils one's goals to acquire, refine, or solidify one's self-concept within early, middle, and late career stages by producing professionally desired outcomes. Using survey instruments to measure role-modelling selection and effectiveness, future research should examine how individuals choose co-culturally competent followers as role models and the effect this type of role model has on career development within national and international arenas. Thus, the proposed research roadmap offers invaluable insights towards better understanding how co-culturally competent followership and role modelling relate to workplace relationships, professional identity, career development as well as individual and organisational goals.

References

Adair, R. (2008). Developing great leaders, one follower at a time. In R. E. Riggio, I. Chaleff, & J. Lipman-Blument (Eds.), *The art of followership: How great followers create great leaders and organizations* (pp. 137–153). San Francisco, CA: Wiley.

Arasaratnam, L. A. (2014). Ten years of research in intercultural communication competence (2003–2013): A retrospective. *Journal of Intercultural Communication, 35*, 5–17.

Avolio, B. C., & Reichard, R. J. (2008). The rise of authentic followership. In R. E. Riggio, I. Chaleff, & J. Lipman-Blument (Eds.), *The art of followership: How great followers create great leaders and organizations* (pp. 25–39). San Francisco, CA: Wiley.

Baker, S. D., Stites-Doe, S. A., Mathis, C. J., & Rosenbach, W. E. (2014). The fluid nature of follower and leader roles. In L. M. Lapierre & M. K. Carsten (Eds.), *Followership: What is it and why do people follow?* (pp. 73–89). Bingley, UK: Emerald Group Publishing.

Bennett, J. M. (2009). Cultivating intercultural competence: A process perspective. In D. K. Deardorff (Ed.), *The SAGE handbook of intercultural competence* (pp. 121–140). Thousand Oaks, CA: SAGE.

Berlo, D. K., Lemert, J. B., & Mertz, R. J. (1969). Dimensions for evaluating the acceptability of message sources. *Public Opinion Quarterly, 33*(4), 563–576.

Carsten, M. K., Harms, P., & Uhl-Bien, M. (2014). Exploring historical perspectives of followership: The need for an expanded view of followers and the follower role. In L. M. Lapierre & M. K. Carsten (Eds.), *Followership: What is it and why do people follow?* (pp. 3–25). Bingley, UK: Emerald Group Publishing.

Carsten, M. K., Uhl-Bien, M., West, B. J., Patera, J. L., & McGregor, R. (2010). Exploring social constructions of followership: A qualitative study. *Leadership Quarterly, 21*(3), 543–562. https://doi.org/10.1016/j.leaqua.2010.03.01.

Carver, C. S., & Scheier, M. F. (1981). *Attention and self-regulation: A control-theory approach to human behavior*. New York, NY: Springer.

Carver, C. S., & Scheier, M. F. (2004). Self-regulation of action and affect. In R. F. Baumeister & K. D. Vohs (Eds.), *Handbook of self-regulation: Research, theory, and applications* (pp. 13–39). New York, NY: Guilford Press.

Dawidziuk, M., Boboryko-Hocazade, J., & Mazur, B. (2012). The intercultural competencies of the managers and organizations in the global world. *Managerial Challenges of the Contemporary Society, 3*, 117–120.

Delia, J. G. (1977). Constructivism and the study of human communication. *Quarterly Journal of Speech, 63*(1), 66–83. https://doi.org/10.1080/00335637709383368.

DeRue, D. S., & Ashford, S. J. (2010). Who will lead and who will follow? A social process of leadership identity construction in organizations.

Academy of Management Review, 35(4), 627–647. https://doi.org/10.5465/AMR.2010.53503267.

de Vignemont, F., & Singer, T. (2006). The empathic brain: How, when and why? *Trends in Cognitive Sciences, 10*(10), 435–441. https://doi.org/10.1016/j.tics.2006.08.008.

Dixon, G. (2008). Getting together. In R. E. Riggio, I. Chaleff, & J. Lipman-Blument (Eds.), *The art of followership: How great followers create great leaders and organizations* (pp. 155–176). San Francisco, CA: Wiley.

Epitropaki, O., Sy, T., Martin, R., Tram-Quon, S., & Topakas, A. (2013). Implicit leadership and followership theories "in the wild": Taking stock of information-processing approaches to leadership and followership in organizational settings. *Leadership Quarterly, 24*(6), 858–881. https://doi.org/10.1016/j.leaqua.2013.10.005.

Fitzsimons, G. M., & Bargh, J. A. (2004). Automatic self-regulation. In K. D. Vohs & R. F. Baumeister (Eds.), *Handbook of self-regulation: Research, theory, and applications* (pp. 151–170). New York, NY: Guilford Press.

Ghosh, R. (2012). Mentors providing challenge and support: Integrating concepts from teacher mentoring in education and organizational mentoring in business. *Human Resource Development Review, 12*(2), 144–176. https://doi.org/10.1177/1534484312465608.

Gibson, D. E. (2003). Developing the professional self-concept: Role model construals in early, middle, and late career stages. *Organization Science, 14*(5), 591–610. https://doi.org/10.1287/orsc.14.5.591.16767.

Gibson, D. E. (2004). Role models in career development: New directions for theory and research. *Journal of Vocational Behavior, 65*(1), 134–156. https://doi.org/10.1016/S0001-8791(03)00051-4.

Goldstein, N. J., Vezich, S., & Shapiro, J. R. (2014). Perceived perspective taking: When others walk in our shoes. *Journal of Personality and Social Psychology, 106*(6), 941–960. https://doi.org/10.1037/1a0036395.

Hecht, M. L. (1993). 2002—A research odyssey: Toward the development of a communication theory of identity. *Communication Monographs, 60*(1), 76–82. https://doi.org/10.1080/03637759309376297.

Hecht, M. L. (2015). Communication theory of identity: Multilayered understandings of performed identities. In D. O. Braithwaite & Paul Schrodt (Eds.), *Engaging theories in interpersonal communication: Multiple perspectives* (pp. 175–187). Thousand Oaks, CA: SAGE.

Hinrichs, K. T., & Hinrichs, A. T. (2014). Comparing followers and subordinates: Accounting for the effects of organizational hierarchy. In L. M. Lapierre

& M. K. Carsten (Eds.), *Followership: What is it and why do people follow?* (pp. 89–105). Bingley, UK: Emerald Group Publishing.

Hogg, M. A., & Terry, D. J. (2000). Social identity and self categorization processes in organizational contexts. *Academy of Management Review, 25*(1), 121–140. https://doi.org/10.5465/AMR.2000.2791606.

Howell, J. P., & Mendez, M. J. (2008). Three perspectives on followership. In R. E. Riggio, I. Chaleff, & J. Lipman-Blument (Eds.), *The art of followership: How great followers create great leaders and organizations* (pp. 25–39). San Francisco, CA: Wiley.

Jaussi, K. S., & Randel, A. E. (2014). Leading to develop truly effective followers. In L. M. Lapierre & M. K. Carsten (Eds.), *Followership: What is it and why do people follow?* (pp. 141–155). Bingley, UK: Emerald Group Publishing Limited.

Junker, N. M., & van Dick, R. (2014). Implicit theories in organizational settings: A systematic review and research agenda of implicit leadership and followership theories. *Leadership Quarterly, 25*(6), 1154–1173. https://doi.org/10.1016/j.leaqua.2014.09.002.

Korsgaard, A. M., Meglino, B. M., Lester, S. W., & Jeong, S. S. (2010). Paying you back or paying me forward: Understanding rewarded and unrewarded organizational citizenship behavior. *Journal of Applied Psychology, 95*(2), 277–290. https://doi.org/10.1037/a0018137.

Kram, K. E. (1985). *Mentoring at work: Developmental relationships in organizational life*. Glenview, IL: Scott, Foresman.

Lockwood, P. L., Seara-Cardoso, A., & Viding, E. (2014). Emotion regulation moderates the association between empathy and prosocial behavior. *Plos ONE, 9*(5), 1–6. https://doi.org/10.1371/journal.pone.0096555.

McCroskey, J. C., & Teven, J. J. (1999). Goodwill: A reexamination of the construct and its measurement. *Communications Monographs, 66*(1), 90–103.

McCroskey, J. C., & Young, T. J. (1981). Ethos and credibility: The construct and its measurement after three decades. *Central States Speech Journal, 32*(1), 24–34. https://doi.org/10.1111/j.1468-2958.1981.tb00657.x.

O'Keefe, D. J., & Sypher, H. E. (1981). Cognitive complexity measures and the relationship of cognitive complexity to communication. *Human Communication Research, 8*(1), 72–92. https://doi.org/10.1111/j.1468-2958.1981.tb00657.x.

Popper, M. (2014). Why do people follow? In L. M. Lapierre & M. K. Carsten (Eds.), *Followership: What is it and why do people follow?* (pp. 109–120). Bingley, UK: Emerald Group Publishing.

Pusch, M. D. (2009). The interculturally competent global leader. In D. K. Deardorff (Ed.), *The SAGE handbook of intercultural competence* (pp. 66–85). Thousand Oaks, CA: SAGE.

Spitzberg, B. H. (2000). A model of intercultural communication competence. In L. A. Samovar, R. E. Porter, E. R. McDaniel, & C. S. Roy (Eds.), *Intercultural communication: A reader* (pp. 379–391). Belmont, CA: Wadsworth.

Spitzberg, B. H., & Changnon, G. (2009). Conceptualizing intercultural competence. In D. K. Deardorff (Ed.), *The SAGE handbook of intercultural competence* (pp. 2–52). Thousand Oaks, CA: SAGE.

Stech, E. L. (2008). A new leadership-followership paradigm. In R. E. Riggio, I. Chaleff, & J. Lipman-Blument (Eds.), *The art of followership: How great followers create great leaders and organizations* (pp. 41–52). San Francisco, CA: Wiley.

Sy, T., & McCoy, T. (2014). Being both leaders and followers: Advancing a model of leader and follower role switching. In L. M. Lapierre & M. K. Carsten (Eds.), *Followership: What is it and why do people follow?* (pp. 73–89). Bingley, UK: Emerald Group Publishing.

Tee, E. Y., Paulsen, N., & Ashkanasy, N. M. (2013). Revisiting followership through a social identity perspective: The role of collective follower emotion and action. *Leadership Quarterly, 24*(6), 902–918. https://doi.org/10.1016/j.leaqua.2013.10.002.

Ting-Toomey, S. (2009). Intercultural conflict competence as a facet of intercultural competence development: Multiple conceptual approaches. In D. K. Deardorff (Ed.), *The SAGE handbook of intercultural competence* (pp. 100–120). Thousand Oaks, CA: SAGE.

Tsui, A. S., & Ashford, S. J. (1994). Adaptive self-regulation: A process view of managerial effectiveness. *Journal of Management, 20*(1), 93–121.

Uhl-Bien, M., Riggio, R. E., Lowe, K. B., & Carsten, M. K. (2014). Followership theory: A review and research agenda. *Leadership Quarterly, 25*(1), 83–104. https://doi.org/10.1016/j.leaqua.2013.11.007.

VanderPal, G., & Ko, V. S. C. (2014). An overview of global leadership: Ethics, values, cultural diversity and conflicts. *Journal of Leadership, Accountability and Ethics, 11*(3), 166–175.

2

Role Modelling and Its Impact on the Self-Development of Academics

Julie Nyanjom

Introduction

The work of the academic in higher education is challenging, given the changes taking place within the higher education environment (Buchanan, Gordon, & Schuck, 2008; Cretchley et al., 2014; De Janasz & Sullivan, 2004; Etzkowitz, 2003; Huyghe & Knockaert, 2015; Karpiak, 2000; Thorsen, 1996). These changes continue to redefine the academic role in higher education and pose challenges to successful attainment of the academic's personal and professional goals. Significant changes include higher expectations of quality research outputs (Seo, Hedayati Mehdiabadi, & Huang, 2016), a gradual shift to learner-centred teaching approaches (Cretchley et al., 2014; Toews & Yazedjian, 2007), higher monitoring of university systems through quality assurance initiatives (Buchanan et al., 2008; Cretchley et al., 2014), and

J. Nyanjom (✉)
Edith Cowan University, Bunbury, Australia
e-mail: j.nyanjom@ecu.edu.au

S. Vidyasagar and P. Hatti (eds.), *Leadership and Role Modelling*,
Palgrave Studies in Leadership and Followership,
https://doi.org/10.1007/978-3-319-69056-8_2

increased expectations to meet internal and external community needs through service activities (Toews & Yazedjian, 2007). There are institutions of higher learning that are moving beyond the traditional goals of simply being knowledge conservationists, to becoming entrepreneurial organisations that strive to be economically and socially self-sustaining (Etzkowitz, 2003; Huyghe & Knockaert, 2015). The changing environment of higher education is escalating the work required from academics and resulting in stress-producing pressures hitherto only experienced in corporate life (Thorsen, 1996). Whilst at one time what constituted the academic profession may have been quite clear, the changing landscape has blurred that clarity (Briggs, 2005; Thorsen, 1996). It is evident that academics may need support to achieve personal and professional development goals. Role modelling is an initiative that may have an impact in this endeavour.

Personal and professional development is the process of achieving competencies and experiences necessary to progress successfully in one's profession. It entails taking deliberate steps to improve oneself and learn new ways of thinking and doing. In the context of this chapter's discussions, personal and professional development will be used interchangeably with self-development, a term that will holistically be understood as an academic's personal initiative to seek growth opportunities by interacting with their environment through role modelling. Additionally, the terms 'academics' and 'professionals' are used interchangeably to mean educators in higher education.

Given that the challenging expectations from academics in higher education propel them to seek self-development objectives and the fact that role models are generally viewed as individuals who inspire others to set ambitious personal and professional goals, it was expected that the notion of self-development would have attracted considerable attention in terms of empirical research. Surprisingly, there is little empirical research addressing role modelling in higher education in general, or personal and professional development of academics in particular. In addition, there is a paucity of empirical research on role models in organisational settings. Understanding how role modelling makes an impact on the self-development of academics is important to explore because such an investigation begins to illuminate the dynamics of role modelling in higher education. The exploration could also lead to the identification of possible interventions at the organisational level that may support the personal and professional development process for academics. Because of the scarcity of empirical research on role modelling specific to academics, this literature review has accessed diverse literature, such as those in organisational science, organisational behaviour, and general education.

This chapter discusses how role modelling presents itself in higher education. It explores how role models in higher education can positively influence the self-development of academics. The chapter begins by discussing definitional issues in role modelling. It then moves to a discussion of the academic profession and how role modelling interfaces with the construction of the academic's professional identity and self-concept. How self-development is achieved through role modelling is then outlined. The chapter concludes with recommendations for practice and suggestions for future research.

Defining Role Modelling

Role modelling has been advanced as having the potential to enhance personal and professional development (Bosma, Hessels, Schutjens, Van Praag, & Verheul, 2012; Gibson, 2003; Ibarra, 1999; Kwan, Mao, & Zhang, 2010; Pratt, Rockmann, & Kaufmann, 2006; Sealy & Singh, 2010; Singh, Vinnicombe, & James, 2006). Despite the general and empirical support for the positive developmental outcomes of role modelling, it remains a concept that has not been definitively defined (Gibson, 2004; Morgenroth, Ryan, & Peters, 2015). Two related terms that are often confused are role modelling and mentoring. Often, researchers use these two terms interchangeably, with the apparent assumption that they mean the same thing, an approach that only adds to the confusion in terms of defining the role-modelling concept. The overlaps between the two terms may be occurring because role modelling is considered a fundamental function of mentoring (Jacobi, 1991; Kram, 1988), meaning that mentors are required to act as role models to their mentees. However, whilst mentoring utilises role modelling as a core function, role modelling can occur without a mentoring intervention. There are therefore distinct differences between these two roles. Allen and Eby (2007) highlight three elements that distinguish role modelling from mentoring. Whilst mentoring requires a certain degree of mutuality, relational closeness, and interaction between participating parties, role modelling does not require any of these elements. Role modelling does not require face-to-face interaction. It is a cognitive concept that is executed in the mind of the individual. To benefit from role modelling, one does not require to build a relationship with another that cultivates trust and friendship. Role modelling involves observable learning, whilst mentoring pre-supposes the intention to offer relational support and guidance. Role models are those individuals that exercise influence over others through their behaviour. They exhibit behavioural attributes that are desirable to others and can contribute to the achievement of desired personal and/or professional goals (Gibson, 2004; Macfarlane, 2011). Specifically, in the higher education environment, role modelling is how an academic *perceives* another as a role model and how they use this perception to lead them to desired self-developmental goals that achieve personal and professional aspirations.

Nature of the Academic Profession

The work of the academic is measured through how they communicate, connect, and collaborate with different audiences. In general, academics are expected to develop a quality research portfolio, achieve excellence in teaching, and network within the institution and the wider community through service roles. In addition, they are expected to have excellent time management and organisational skills. Executing these often conflicting tasks is challenging, as it requires a diverse range of competencies (Briggs, 2005; De Janasz & Sullivan, 2004; Seo et al., 2016; Thorsen, 1996; Toews & Yazedjian, 2007). In a study conducted using women academics, Seo et al. (2016) identified six core competencies academics need for a successful career in higher education—making important connections, fulfilling responsibilities in higher education, being politically savvy, managing personal and professional obligations, developing a sense of self-agency for one's career, and believing in oneself in the work environment (see Table 2.1). These competencies provide a good representation of what academics do and therefore include aspects of what they may desire to enhance as self-development goals.

Table 2.1 Core career competencies for academics

Core competency	Sub-category
Making important connections	1. Building professional networks 2. Nurturing built networks 3. Finding people who support you inside/outside your department 4. Seeking role models and mentor(s) to guide you
Fulfilling responsibilities in academia	1. Conducting research for publication 2. Applying for grants and projects 3. Attending to your instruction 4. Contributing to your department
Being politically savvy	1. Considering politics in every aspect a. Seeking political supporters (alliances) b. Considering politics in writing c. Considering politics in general 2. Being your own advocate
Managing personal and professional obligations	1. Balancing work and life 2. Developing organisational skills a. Prioritising your time b. Following a strict sense of your short-term and long-term goals 3. Knowing your possibility and limit 4. Building a supportive relationship with your partner
Developing a sense of self-agency for your career	1. Matching your interest with career choices 2. Strategically setting your career goals 3. Continuously pursuing your career 4. Taking advantage of opportunities 5. Building realistic backup plans
Believing in yourself in the work environment	1. Positive attitude towards self 2. Dealing with gender-based expectations towards females from both colleagues and students

Source Adapted from Seo et al. (2016, p. 9)

The competencies that inform the academic profession can provide clues to the attributes academics may seek for emulation from prospective role models.

For many academics in higher education, the academic profession is a vocation that necessitates lifelong learning, and freedom to navigate their professional journey. Once they join higher education, the expectation is that academics will hit the ground running and maintain an upward trajectory, or to express it more accurately, maintain a juggling act of various projects (De Janasz & Sullivan, 2004), that propel them to progressively higher levels in the institution for the duration of their career. In general, other than programmed teaching assignments, academics have the freedom to work on projects of their choosing. But with this freedom comes isolation for many, where nobody knows or cares about what one is working on or if one is working at all (Karpiak, 2000). Personal and professional development is often left up to the individual academic. Those who accomplish success pour in time and effort to achieve planned self-development goals. With such effort comes the desire to provide work that has high impact and brings recognition and validation. Academics take pride in showcasing their achievements and it is through these successes that they often become visible to others in their social contexts.

The wide range of competencies required for effective teaching, research, and service in a continually changing university environment makes it challenging for academics to receive adequate formal training in aspects of their work (De Janasz & Sullivan, 2004). Thus, as academic roles become more challenging, the need for personal and professional development becomes more critical. In an effort to meet and surpass expectations, academics tend to spread themselves too thin, tackling various projects or roles simultaneously, debating the 'right' choices of professional service activities to undertake, continually searching for avenues to enhance their teaching practice, and managing the 'publish or perish' culture of higher education in a highly competitive publishing environment. It is possible that academics could mitigate these challenges by utilising the role-modelling process for self-development. Role modelling can be an intervention that could assist academics better execute their self-development agenda and achieve aspirations of the kind of professional they wish to become.

Professional Identity and Self-Concept

The conceptualisation of a viable professional identity is fundamental to self-development (Gibson, 2003; Ibarra, 1999; Singh et al., 2006). Ibarra (1999) defines professional identity as an enduring set of attributes, beliefs, values, motives, and experiences by which people define themselves. Identity, in this chapter's context, refers to the perceptive meaning people attach to the different roles they play as they interact with others in different settings (McCall & Simmons, 1978; Stryker, 1980). These roles they play are attached to the work they perform. A professional academic identity, therefore, encompasses the attributes perceived by the academic as depicting the type of professional they are and can become.

Integral to the process of constructing one's professional identity is the refining of one's self-concept. A person's self-concept is how one views themselves in relation to others within their social context at both personal and professional levels (Super, 1980). What an academic believes about themselves is important because how they see themselves defines their professional identity. The academic's professional identity is not static and will evolve in response to changing work roles (Gibson, 2003). Given the nature of their profession, it is difficult for academics to separate the personal from the professional self. In pursuit of professional objectives, the social and emotional aspects of the journey intertwine into one intentional aspiration. As they journey through their professional lives, academics make personal choices on how to construct their professional identity. For example, academics may decide to focus more on research activities than on teaching, or desire to establish an effective work–life balance. As the academic begins to chart the path of their professional career, they progressively build their self-concept. This journey involves a cognitive process about their professional aspirations and a vision of who they want to become. Role models can provide a vision of who a professional could be in future.

The notion of possible selves (Markus & Nurius, 1986) assists in the understanding of how a professional may think about different visions of themselves in their quest to construct their ideal professional identity. Ideas of who the academic visualises they could be lead them to scan their environment for possible role models who may provide tangible clues on how to achieve their predetermined self-development range of competencies. Bucher and Stelling's (1977) concept of partial role models explains the potential for academics to access several role models at the same time as they search for attributes that may fulfil their perceived identity. The theory suggests that observers, depending on their self-development needs, will be attracted by specific attributes in different role models. These attributes can then be emulated and will contribute to the building of the desired identity. Professionals, therefore, utilise multiple role models to construct their ideal self, by imitating observed bits from each role model they perceive to be relevant to them. For example, an academic may wish to enhance their research agenda, and at the same time, they may want to be a more effective teacher. Depending on the specific situation, and the competencies sought, these two visions may call for various role models within the academic's social circles to fulfil desired developmental needs.

Ibarra's (1999) empirical research advanced the notions of the significance of possible selves and partial role models in the construction of the professional identity, followed more recently by other studies supporting the fact that role modelling contributes to the construction of one's self-concept. Ibarra (1999) studied managers in the early stages of their careers and established that less experienced managers constructed various 'provisional selves' by observing and adapting their role model's professional traits and styles to suit their targeted self-development objectives. Gibson (2003) found that professionals utilised several role models throughout their careers, the emphasis of their emulation changing only in relevance to the identification of which attributes from role models would reinforce their professional self-concept. Similarly, Singh et al. (2006) found that professional women accessed a variety of role models in their endeavour to construct their ideal professional identity, drawing relevant attributes from each role model as desired. The role-modelling process, therefore, suggests that the academic will need to seek various role models from whom they can emulate attributes that contribute to the achievement of their planned self-development goals. A portfolio of role models allows an observer to experiment with different possible selves in their endeavour to construct their professional identity (Bucher & Stelling, 1977; Ibarra, 1999).

In sum, in providing self-development benefits, role modelling plays two distinct roles. The process presents 'role expectations', communicating an 'I want to be like you' message, thus assisting in the shaping of an academic's professional identity. Second, the process presents 'modelling expectations', thereby contributing to the development and enhancement of the academic's self-concept. As will be discussed later, these roles influence the selection process of role models. At the same time, the professional identity construction and the gradual enhancement of one's self-concept impact how the academic progressively manage their self-development as they advance through their career.

Self-Development and Career Advancement

The rationale for self-development emanates from a natural expectation for professional career progression. Once they join higher education, academics are expected to progressively move from one stage to another following a well-established promotion track. This progression is driven by self-developmental objectives as articulated by the individual academic and guided by institutional expectations.

Role models play a significant function in guiding professionals achieve their aspirations (Bucher & Stelling, 1977; Gibson, 2003; Ibarra, 1999). The sparse research on role modelling in organisations focuses on the development of professionals in the early stages of their careers and marginalised groups such as women and culturally diverse professionals, giving the impression that only such professionals need role modelling for self-development (see, e.g. Gibson, 2006; Kachchaf, Ko, Hodari, & Ong, 2015; Singh et al., 2006; Terosky, O'Meara, & Campbell, 2014). However, a study conducted by Gibson (2003) found all employees, regardless of their age or career stage, access role models to progressively enhance their self-concept. In addition, Creswell and Brown (1992) studied academic leaders in higher education and established that the leaders recognised they were role models not only to academics in the early stages of their careers but also to all academics, regardless of the stage they were in their career. Gibson's (2003) study advanced that a professional's need to observe and emulate role models does not change as they grow older and progress through their career. Rather, what changes is the specificity of the attributes professionals seek from their identified role models. This implies that the process of using role models for self-development becomes more refined as professionals become more comfortable with who they are. Literature thus suggests that (a) self-development can be enhanced by attending role models throughout one's career and (b) older, more experienced, academics not only are potential role models, but also seek role models themselves. Consequently, the early, middle, and late career stages attract different self-development strategies depending on the professional's evolving needs.

In the early stages, new faculty struggle with adaptation and orientation (Creswell & Brown, 1992), a situation that is exacerbated by the 'sink or swim' culture inherent in most higher education institutions. Each academic joins higher education as an expert in their own right. This fact, however, does not diminish the self-doubt and feelings of insufficiency that often afflicts academics in the early stages of their careers. Academics are left to self-manage assigned tasks and other institutional expectations. In this environment, the requirement for self-development quickly sets in. In this time of socialisation, professionals pay attention to role models to create a viable self-concept (Gibson, 2003; Ibarra, 1999). During this career stage, role models can play a significant part in the academic's socialisation.

In middle-career stages, academics re-examine their careers which may have plateaued (Creswell & Brown, 1992; Terosky et al., 2014). Many mid-career academics are usually middle-aged (Karpiak, 2000), and for them, it is a time to redefine their style and reaffirm their professional objectives, thus refining their self-concept (Gibson, 2003). It is potentially also a time for renewed commitment and job satisfaction (Karpiak, 2000). At this time, self-development needs have changed and academics may have a need for personal and professional development (Karpiak, 2000). But this is also the time when institutions assume these mid-career academics have little need for professional development and offer little support to meet their developmental needs.

The middle-career stage is a period where professionals often perceive the absence of relevant role models and cite this lack of role models as a barrier to career advancement (Singh et al., 2006). At this stage, the number of potential role models narrows because mid-career professionals become much more selective in the attributes they perceive as relevant from role models (Gibson, 2003).

Late-stage academics also have professional developmental goals they would like to achieve, with senior professors exhibiting changing interests (Creswell & Brown, 1992). At this stage of their career, senior academics may need exposure to role models who can assist them achieve specific organisational skills (Gibson, 2003), perhaps brought about by technological and other environmental changes occurring in higher education. Older professionals generally seek to enhance and affirm their self-concept (Gibson, 2003). Availability of role models that align with desired needs can enhance the commitment and satisfaction levels of these mature academics to the extent that they continue to provide essential benefits to the organisation.

Given the nature of the academic profession, the notion that all academics seek role models through the entire span of their professional career aligns well with how self-development would manifest in higher education. With the requirement to be continuously learning as a fundamental part of the profession, it is expected that new competencies will need to be developed depending on different situations. It is presumed, therefore, that academics will utilise role modelling as a developmental intervention throughout their professional career. Since role models will be accessed at different stages of the professional journey, and for varied attributes depending on current self-development needs, the selection of role models becomes critical to the achievement of self-development goals.

Selection of Role Models for Self-Development

Selecting role models is a unique and personal choice that is a process of social comparison (Collins, 1996) and has to fulfil certain conditions within the mind of the observer. Role models need to be perceived as relevant and in alignment with the observer's current and future goals (Lockwood & Kunda, 1997). Relevance, in this case, can adopt the views of two theoretical constructs. The first theoretical construct follows role identity theory (McCall & Simmons, 1978; Stryker, 1980) and suggests that an academic may be guided by similarities in motives and characteristics, including demographic characteristics such as gender, race, or values. The selection process focuses on the role aspects of role modelling and is driven by the heady motivation to own an aspect of the role model. The ability to be attracted to and influenced by others within their social contexts can be explained through Byrne's (1971) similarity-attraction theory which explores the concept that people are usually attracted to those similar to themselves. This view is supported by the homophily concept, which explains why people will often identify with those who are like them in certain ways (Ibarra, 1992). Literature highlights, for example, that women academics (Gibson, 2006; Terosky et al., 2014) and academics from culturally diverse backgrounds (Kachchaf et al., 2015) have fewer role models because these marginalised groups struggle to identify role models aligned with their values (Kachchaf et al., 2015; Sealy & Singh, 2010; Singh et al., 2006; Terosky et al., 2014). The motivational power a professional may feel in observing another professional perceived to be similar to themselves in relevant ways accomplish what once seemed unattainable can result in an 'if they can do it, so can I' inspiration that can make goals appear realistic and achievable.

The second theoretical construct follows Bandura's (1977, 1986) theory of social learning, where an academic could be guided by cognitive patterns they wish to access such as experience and relevant professional acumen they observe in the role model. In this case, the selection process focuses on the modelling aspects of the role-modelling concept, highlighting the specifics the professional can learn from the role model. The academic would then be attracted to professionals who can assist them in learning specific desired competencies.

In consideration of the above literature and the nature of the academic profession earlier discussed, there are unique reasons that may impact the selection of role models for self-developmental outcomes. First, academics will most likely find their role models essentially within higher education. This is owing to the specificity of potential self-development objectives which border around research, teaching, and service—competencies that are quite industry-specific. In higher education, given the context in which academics gain exposure, those academics who have published more, who display quality teaching behaviour, and who have exemplary service records will most likely be identified by other academics as role models.

Second, academics will most likely access a wide spectrum of role models for emulation (Gibson, 2004; Ibarra, 1999; Singh et al., 2006), to seek partial role models (Bucher & Stelling, 1977) who can provide targeted skills, attributes, and professional styles that academics can then adapt to create unique professional identities. Academics can access role models to avoid negative behaviour as well (Gibson, 2004; Ibarra, 1999; Lockwood & Kunda, 1999). Whilst positive role models will motivate observers to strive to achieve modelled behaviour, negative role models will motivate observers to avoid failure. Therefore, those role models who indicate how 'not' to do things may be just as valuable to personal and professional development as those with positive messages.

Third, in higher education, role models will permeate through all levels of the organisation. Academics who have proved successful in different aspects of higher education have high potential to be role models, regardless of their position within the institution. Kram and Isabella (1985) suggested that a role model is often more senior in terms of career stages. In contrast, Gibson (2004) suggests that seniority within the role-modelling concept is outdated, in effect implying that an academic does not necessarily have to be senior to be a role model. Having said this, however, role modelling is supported by accumulated experience, which often comes with many years of practice (Kram, 1988). It is anticipated that being viewed as a role model in higher education will go with the territory of experience and professional acumen rather than seniority. This means that role models will tend to be experienced members of higher education, especially those who hold leadership portfolios whilst pursuing exemplary research and teaching records (Macfarlane, 2011). The more experienced academics, with proven and public records, will attract observation and emulation from their colleagues.

In discussing the selection of role models in higher education, it is opportune to highlight the potential for academics to make themselves available as role models. The work academics do is often visible to others, and with this comes the opportunity to be observed and emulated. Academics have the opportunity to project their professional identity through role modelling. Through their actions, academics demonstrate observable clues to others of who they are. Through this avenue, more experienced academic role models influence other academics to advance the development of their own unique professional identity. Literature does support the fact that invariably more experienced academics will desire to be perceived as role models by their colleagues (Cretchley et al., 2014; Juntrasook, 2014; Kachchaf et al., 2015; Macfarlane, 2011). How experienced academics value aspects of their work will permeate through to role-modelling behaviour. There are academics who make concerted efforts to demarcate what they most want to be modelled for. For example, a study by Cretchley et al. (2014) found that most senior academics would rather display positive role-modelling behaviours for research activities than for teaching. Accepting the utility of role modelling can provide self-development outcomes to both the observed and observing professionals, as well as benefits for the organisation. It is argued that becoming aware of the influence one has on others and how their behaviour acts as a conduit to behavioural change in others may encourage one to be a more deliberate and influential role model.

In the final analysis, the choice of acceptable role models lies with the individual academic. If the academic scans their environment and perceives that no one aligns with their values, they will conclude there is no one relevant to emulate and will perceive a shortage of role models. The perceived lack of relevant role models may be detrimental to the academic's pursuit of self-development goals. At the organisational level, the objective of utilising role modelling as a professional development intervention would be to initiate strategies that strive to make available adequate role models for all academics. It is only through the successful identification and selection of appropriate role models that anticipated self-development outcomes can potentially be achieved.

Self-Development Through Role Modelling

Social learning theory (Bandura, 1977, 1986) provides theoretical support for the concept of self-development by advancing the notion that people can learn from observing and emulating role models. At a personal level, a professional can assess the benefits in the environment that may accrue from new learning and deliberately select behaviour that will lead them to achieve self-determined developmental goals. Modelling offers a continuous and broad spectrum of learning opportunities where the new learning can be applied to different circumstances as required. When the less experienced academic identifies with a role model, recognises attributes that are admirable, and can assess functional value from adopting this new behaviour, role modelling can accord an opportunity for the process of learning to occur effectively, and the objectives of self-development to be achieved.

The act of role modelling has attracted little research attention. Ibarra (1999) found that professionals emulate role models in different ways, depending on what behaviour the professional perceives will positively contribute to their development. In this research, Ibarra did not clarify what role models actually do to engage with the process of role modelling. Gibson (2004, p. 135) confirms that 'little research has examined the processes by which individuals perceive, create and sustain development through identification with role models'. It is therefore not clearly understood what a role model does or should do to execute or initiate a developmental intervention in an academic setting. The lack of research has blurred the distinction between role models as individuals and role modelling as an action. What is known, however, is that observing role models can result in the learning of particular skills and behaviours (Bosma et al., 2012; Gibson, 2003; Ibarra, 1999; Kwan et al., 2010; Pratt et al., 2006; Sealy & Singh, 2010; Singh et al., 2006).

Learning from role models means observing their behaviours and emulating desirable attributes. However, observation in itself is not adequate to result in the achievement of self-developmental outcomes. Role models become effective in self-development when the observer perceives them as relevant. When considered relevant, role models can have both motivational and inspirational effects (Lockwood & Kunda, 1997). Consequently, the process of self-development through role modelling combines motivation—individuals aspire to be like the role model in some way, and imitation—individuals adopt and mimic behaviours and style from the role model until they find the right fit. Thus, motivation and imitation are fundamental components of the role-modelling process that impact the achievement of self-development goals.

Professionals are motivated by role models who encourage strategies that align with their developmental inspirations (Bosma et al., 2012; Gibson, 2004; Lockwood & Kunda, 1997; Morgenroth et al., 2015). Role models affirm to the observer that they are not alone in their belief of who they aspire to be. Motivation plays a fundamental role in self-development when observers believe that the higher goals they are observing are attainable (Lockwood & Kunda, 1997). The realisation that certain professional goals are achievable because someone else has attained them, and illustration through modelling behaviour of how tasks can be achieved, inspires motivation to strive to achieve similar developmental goals. In addition, observing these role models authenticates organisational expectations and potential to achieve set professional objectives. Through this realisation, the academic can visualise a possible future self (Markus & Nurius, 1986). The motivational force that results from this process acts as a catalyst to the learning process (Morgenroth et al., 2015) and has the potential to push the academic to take control of their self-development through self-direction. As they attempt to emulate the role model, professionals continue to define their self-concept and refine their professional identity (Gibson, 2003).

The learning in the role-modelling process is adopted through imitation (Ibarra, 1999). Acquiring behavioural skills involves more than observation and requires experimentation (Bandura, 1977). Experimentation is done through imitation (Ibarra, 1999) and is a process that involves looking through one's repertoire of role models and mimicking individual traits that align with the desired self-concept. As they observe their identified role models, the academic becomes more aware of intricate aspects of their self-image. Through the process of imitation, the academic's personal values are shaped, and their sense of professional identity reinforced. Ibarra (1999), in examining how new professional roles shape professional identity, found that the adaptation process involves observing role models to identify potential identities, experimenting with these possible selves, and evaluating the provisional self to establish alignment with professional expectations.

The discussion above provides a compelling case for role modelling as a self-development intervention in higher education. Clearly, role modelling has high potential to contribute significantly to the achievement of positive self-development outcomes for academics in higher education and assist them to manage their professional identities within a turbulent environment. The facilitation and support of higher education institutions can enhance this self-development process.

Recommendations for Practice

This chapter has revealed that role modelling can indeed be an effective self-development activity in higher education. There is a need for institutions of higher education to recognise the changing role of academics and initiate appropriate professional development approaches to support their work (Briggs, 2005; Cretchley et al., 2014; Macfarlane, 2011). Academics need support to achieve expected outcomes if they are to thrive in higher education. The need to proactively provide facilitation and support for the self-development of academics is critical if institutions are to maximise the full potential of academics and align it to the changing landscape of academia. Institutions of higher learning should cultivate an environment that encourages associations with a wide variety of people that can contribute to personal and professional development. Given the nature of the academic profession, and the autonomy that is an essential part of self-development, role modelling is an intervention that should receive more attention in higher education than it has in the past.

Institutions of higher education can play a greater role in encouraging experienced academics to be role models. Regardless of the approach adopted by institutions, taking advantage of role modelling as a developmental initiative for academics assumes there would be systems and policies in place to support such an endeavour. Research, however, indicates that often, institutional systems and policies do not overtly support role-modelling objectives (Juntrasook, 2014; Macfarlane, 2011). A study carried out by Macfarlane (2011) revealed that predominantly senior academics feel underutilised in terms of the developmental objectives of less experienced colleagues. Whilst the more experienced academics were willing to share more of their skills and expertise, institutional systems and policies were making this more difficult. A review of institutional systems is essential to ensure policies and procedures support the facilitation of role-modelling initiatives.

Role modelling as an approach to professional development should not involve excessive control. There should be autonomy for the academic to drive their own self-development. The essence of role modelling as a developmental intervention comes from observation and emulation by less experienced academics. A well-oiled institutional mechanism means there would be systems in place to support professional development that is desired by academics. In institutions, where more experienced academics engage in their own observable professional development and activities, less experienced academics would be able to observe and emulate appropriate behaviour that suits their individual and unique paths for self-development.

It could be useful for institutions of higher learning to consider deliberate developmental initiatives that accentuate and provide opportunities for role modelling for less experienced academics. One way could be to facilitate the establishment of formal and informal networks which would have potential to expose potential role models akin to the mentor networks proposed by Higgins and Kram (2001). The developmental network of mentors proposed by Higgins and Kram is composed of a set of people supporting and guiding a single mentee through career advancement. Similarly, the notion of a network of role models to guide an academic could be encouraged in organisational settings. This idea is supported by the theory of partial role models (Bucher & Stelling, 1977) as a natural process of selecting relevant role models. Academics could be encouraged to access numerous role models, composed of professionals distant or in close proximity to the academic, who could be actively involved in the academic's professional development activities (such as co-authorship), or passively emulated from afar.

Second, exposing the exemplary works of academics through varied networking opportunities and informative seminars could assist academics access role models relevant to their self-development goals. This approach can also make it easier for academics to connect with more experienced colleagues working on related areas and may lead to opportunities for collaboration on projects of interest (e.g. as co-authors or co-supervisors). Establishing connections that result in partnerships has the potential to utilise the essence of role modelling at a deeper and more personal level, where the impact on the achievement of self-development goals would be more powerful. O'Meara and Stromquist (2015) present a case, where role modelling was enhanced through the formation of peer networks amongst academics. Although this study was targeted at women academics, it is an initiative that could work for all academics regardless of gender. In this case study, safe and autonomous spaces that exposed academics to potential role models within higher education were created. Such an initiative has the potential to be based on technology, with networks being developed online and participation being encouraged in different ways.

Third, providing experiential learning situations such as social staff events and opportunities for corridor conversations is another ideal way for potential role models to interact with others. This could provide an opportunity to socialise and share ideas, stimulating intellectual interest by getting to know what other colleagues are thinking, planning, and doing. These face-to-face opportunities could not only effectively contribute to breaking the feelings of isolation experienced by many academics, but also assist academics to rationalise the relevance of role models. The learning spaces created have potential to encourage interaction between colleagues and expose potential role models.

The initiatives presented above call for academics to be proactive in their quest for self-development. These opportunities to observe their more experienced colleagues are not exhaustive, and many more opportunities to connect academics with potential role models could be initiated and adopted. There is, however, a need for more research into the role-modelling concept in academia. For example, research confirming the value of role models to academics could assist in the design of interventions that more specifically target the needs and aspirations of academics. In addition, there is scope for much more work to be done on role modelling in higher education, including studies on the inter-relations between age, career competencies, organisational expectations, and career advancement of academics.

Conclusions

These are turbulent times for institutions of higher learning as they struggle to reposition themselves in the context of changes taking place in the external and internal environments (Etzkowitz, 2003; Huyghe & Knockaert, 2015). Academics are in need of ways of self-development to deal with the changing landscape of higher education. In this environment, role modelling is a possible self-development intervention that can be utilised. The importance of role models lies in the fact that they help academics create their own unique professional identities. This is because observing more experienced colleagues can contribute to the creation and achievement of self-development goals that can then be experimented upon to help construct desired self-concepts that portray to the academic who they want to be. Support for academics is required to assist them in actively exploring role modelling for the benefit of self-development. The impact of access to appropriate role models and how this impact influences the personal and professional development of academics should not be underestimated.

References

Allen, T. D., & Eby, L. T. (2007). Overview and introduction. In T. D. Allen & L. T. Eby (Eds.), *The Blackwell handbook of mentoring: A multiple perspectives approach* (pp. 3–22). Malden, MA: Blackwell.

Bandura, A. (1977). *Social learning theory.* Englewood Cliffs, NJ: Prentice-Hall.

Bandura, A. (1986). *Social foundations of thought and action: A social cognitive perspective*. Englewood Cliffs, NJ: Princeton-Hall.

Bosma, N., Hessels, J., Schutjens, V., Van Praag, M., & Verheul, I. (2012). Entrepreneurship and role models. *Journal of Economic Psychology, 33*(2), 410–424.

Briggs, S. (2005). Changing roles and competencies of academics. *Active Learning in Higher Education, 6*(3), 256–268.

Buchanan, J., Gordon, S., & Schuck, S. (2008). From mentoring to monitoring: The impact of changing work environments on academics in Australian universities. *Journal of Further and Higher Education, 32*(3), 241–250.

Bucher, R., & Stelling, J. G. (1977). *Becoming professional*. Beverly Hills, CA: SAGE.

Byrne, D. (1971). *The attraction paradigm*. Orlando, FL: Academic Press.

Collins, R. L. (1996). For better or worse: The impact of upward social comparison on self-evaluations. *Psychological Bulletin, 119*(1), 51–69.

Creswell, J. W., & Brown, M. L. (1992). How chairpersons enhance faculty research: A grounded theory study. *The Review of Higher Education, 16*(1), 41–62.

Cretchley, P. C., Edwards, S. L., O'Shea, P., Sheard, J., Hurst, J., & Brookes, W. (2014). Research and/or learning and teaching: A study of Australian professors' priorities, beliefs and behaviours. *Higher Education Research & Development, 33*(4), 649–669.

De Janasz, S. C., & Sullivan, S. E. (2004). Multiple mentoring in academe: Developing the professorial network. *Journal of Vocational Behavior, 64*(2), 263–283.

Etzkowitz, H. (2003). Research groups as 'quasi-firms': The invention of the entrepreneurial university. *Research Policy, 32*(1), 109–121.

Gibson, D. E. (2003). Developing the professional self-concept: Role model construals in early, middle, and late career stages. *Organization Science, 14*(5), 591–610.

Gibson, D. E. (2004). Role models in career development: New directions for theory and research. *Journal of Vocational Behavior, 65*(1), 134–156.

Gibson, S. K. (2006). Mentoring of women faculty: The role of organizational politics and culture. *Innovative Higher Education, 31*(1), 63–79.

Higgins, M. C., & Kram, K. E. (2001). Reconceptualizing mentoring at work: A developmental network perspective. *Academy of Management Review, 26*(2), 264–288.

Huyghe, A., & Knockaert, M. (2015). The influence of organizational culture and climate on entrepreneurial intentions among research scientists. *The Journal of Technology Transfer, 40*(1), 138–160.

Ibarra, H. (1992). Homophily and differential returns: Sex differences in network structure and access in an advertising firm. *Administrative Science Quarterly, 37*(3), 422–447.

Ibarra, H. (1999). Provisional selves: Experimenting with image and identity in professional adaptation. *Administrative Science Quarterly, 44*(4), 764–791.

Jacobi, M. (1991). Mentoring and undergraduate academic success: A literature review. *Review of Educational Research, 61*(4), 505–532.

Juntrasook, A. (2014). 'You do not have to be the boss to be a leader': Contested meanings of leadership in higher education. *Higher Education Research & Development, 33*(1), 19–31.

Kachchaf, R., Ko, L., Hodari, A., & Ong, M. (2015). Career–life balance for women of color: Experiences in science and engineering academia. *Journal of Diversity in Higher Education, 8*(3), 175–191.

Karpiak, I. (2000). The 'second call': Faculty renewal and recommitment at midlife. *Quality in Higher Education, 6*(2), 125–134. https://doi.org/10.1080/713692741.

Kram, K. (1988). *Mentoring at work: Developmental relationships in organisational life*. New York, NY: University Press of America.

Kram, K. E., & Isabella, L. (1985). Mentoring alternatives: The role of peer relationships in career development. *Academy of Management Journal, 28*(1), 110–132.

Kwan, H. K., Mao, Y., & Zhang, H. (2010). The impact of role modeling on protégés' personal learning and work-to-family enrichment. *Journal of Vocational Behavior, 77*(2), 313–322.

Lockwood, P., & Kunda, Z. (1997). Superstars and me: Predicting the impact of role models on the self. *Journal of Personality and Social Psychology, 73*(1), 91–103.

Lockwood, P., & Kunda, Z. (1999). Increasing the salience of one's best selves can undermine inspiration by outstanding role models. *Journal of Personality and Social Psychology, 76*(2), 214–228.

Macfarlane, B. (2011). Professors as intellectual leaders: Formation, identity and role. *Studies in Higher Education, 36*(1), 57–73.

Markus, H., & Nurius, P. (1986). Possible selves. *American Psychologist, 41*(9), 954–969.

McCall, G. J., & Simmons, J. L. (1978). *Identities and interactions: An examination of human associations in everyday life*. New York, NY: Free Press.

Morgenroth, T., Ryan, M. K., & Peters, K. (2015). The motivational theory of role modeling: How role models influence role aspirants' goals. *Review of General Psychology, 19*(4), 465–483.

O'Meara, K., & Stromquist, N. P. (2015). Faculty peer networks: Role and relevance in advancing agency and gender equity. *Gender and Education, 27*(3), 338–358.

Pratt, M. G., Rockmann, K. W., & Kaufmann, J. B. (2006). Constructing professional identity: The role of work and identity learning cycles in the customization of identity among medical residents. *Academy of Management Journal, 49*(2), 235–262.

Sealy, R. H., & Singh, V. (2010). The importance of role models and demographic context for senior women's work identity development. *International Journal of Management Reviews, 12*(3), 284–300.

Seo, G. E., Hedayati Mehdiabadi, A., & Huang, W. (2016). Identifying core competencies to advance female professors' careers: An exploratory study in United States academia. *Journal of Further and Higher Education*, 1–19. https://doi.org/10.1080/0309877X.2016.1177167.

Singh, V., Vinnicombe, S., & James, K. (2006). Constructing a professional identity: How young female managers use role models. *Women in Management Review, 21*(1), 67–81.

Stryker, S. (1980). *Symbolic interactionism: A social structural version*. Menlo Park, CA: Benjamin-Cummings.

Super, D. E. (1980). A life-span, life-space approach to career development. *Journal of Vocational Behavior, 16*(3), 282–298.

Terosky, A. L., O'Meara, K., & Campbell, C. M. (2014). Enabling possibility: Women associate professors' sense of agency in career advancement. *Journal of Diversity in Higher Education, 7*(1), 58.

Thorsen, E. J. (1996). Stress in academe: What bothers professors? *Higher Education, 31*(4), 471–489.

Toews, M. L., & Yazedjian, A. (2007). The three-ring circus of academia: How to become the ringmaster. *Innovative Higher Education, 32*(2), 113–122.

3

Role Modelling as an Alternative to Mentoring for Career Development Outcomes in Organisations

Tanjia M. Coleman

Introduction

In previous studies, peer relationships have been considered as an alternative to mentoring relationships; however, they still require a pairing-up model (Kram & Isabella, 1985). The limited research available on role modelling looks to determine the level of understanding within role modelling from three perspectives: Leadership role modelling, direct supervisor role modelling, and peer role modelling. A greater understanding of these three levels of role modelling in the workplace can help determine whether the outcomes of role modelling have a negative or positive effect, as well as the drivers of such outcomes. The outcomes of role modelling can be viewed from two perspectives: sustained career positioning and upward career mobility. Once the outcomes of role modelling are properly explored, models can be created to assist employees in the workplace.

T. M. Coleman (✉)
Reimagine Organization Development, Inc., IL, USA
e-mail: tanjia7@sbcglobal.net

S. Vidyasagar and P. Hatti (eds.), *Leadership and Role Modelling*,
Palgrave Studies in Leadership and Followership,
https://doi.org/10.1007/978-3-319-69056-8_3

This chapter focuses on role modelling and mentorship in the workplace and their impact on diverse senior leaders and middle-management employees as antecedents for career sustainability and/or upward career mobility. Currently, there is a lack of focus on role modelling in corporations, and the focus remains on creating both informal and formal mentoring programmes, although role modelling can be a less evasive and cost-restrictive programme for organisations of any size, owing to not having any stated work or commitment from either participant.

Through a qualitative (interview) approach, this chapter seeks to answer how role modelling is executed, how role modelling can shape organisations in the future and how those involved in role modelling can communicate the benefits and impact of role modelling in the workplace, while differentiating it from mentoring, which can be a much more rigid and organised process. In addition, analysis from the qualitative study described in this chapter will provide insight into role modelling as: (a) a less formalised process that can have greater or similar impact, (b) a more cost-effective model for professional development, and (c) an opportunity to reach more participants. Furthermore, a framework for role modelling is introduced as a means for leaders to understand the impact, influence, and validity of role modelling as a means for upward career mobility.

Review of Literature

The review of literature and discussion that follows focuses on defining both mentoring and role modelling, the differences between mentoring and role modelling, and the evolution of role modelling, as well as impact of close and distant role modelling on the protégé. It highlights considerations such as gender and rank/level within an organisation, as well as the outcomes of mentoring and role modelling for organisations.

Much of academic research has focused on mentoring and mentoring relationships in the workplace as the antecedent to role modelling. According to the Social Science index, the number of mentoring articles during 1977–2007 increased from 1 to 300 in a 30-year span (McDonald, Erickson, & Gatlin, 2009). Role modelling, on the other hand, is thought to be a much more fluid and subjective activity, where it has been deemed difficult—if not impossible—to track progression.

Furthermore, the traditional idea of a role model, as defined from a career construct, is that of a person in an influential role, such as a supervisor or leader, within the organisation. However, role modelling has been deemed critical to the development and upward trajectory of career professionals, although the research is extremely limited in these areas (Gibson, 2003b; Hader, 2007). Terms such as 'informal mentoring' are used interchangeably in relation to role modelling. Informal mentorships are those where both individuals are voluntary participants who select each other for a relationship (Allen, Eby, & Lentz, 2006).

Formal mentoring programmes in organisations continue to gain traction and support across organisations, despite the fact that formal mentoring programmes have limited empirical research regarding outcomes (Allen et al., 2006). Mentoring programmes have been identified as the catalyst for increased representation of women and minorities in organisations. Data from the United States show that women and minorities who participate in formal mentoring programmes make up between 9% and 24% of those in mentoring programmes (Dobbin & Kalev, 2016). However, only about 10% of organisations in the United States have formal mentoring programmes (Dobbin & Kalev, 2016). The characteristics of role modelling and mentoring are different in terms of desired outcomes and approach. Role modelling is defined as 'identification and social comparison' while a mentor is thought to be 'interactive and involved' (Gibson, 2003b). The two can be described by reviewing Table 3.1.

Table 3.1 Role model versus mentor

	Role model	Mentor
Defining processes	Identification and social comparison, which is based on perceived similarity and desire to increase similarity by the individual	Interaction and involvement, which is based on an active interest in and action to advance the individual's career
Potential number	Multiple; observer/follower seeks variety	Typically one or two (primary)
Attributes sought in the target by the observer	Role expectations; definition of self-concept	Career functions; psychosocial functions
Awareness	Typically one way: on the part of the observer	Usually explicit: awareness by both parties

Source Gibson (2003b)

A review of the literature identifies emerging trends in role modelling as a developmental construct in career progression. Positive role modelling occurs when one distinguishes the role model as having a prevalence of attributes that the protégé would consider positive (Gibson, 2003b). In the past, protégés were taught to avoid negative role models; however, a new perspective has been formed regarding negative role models in that they indeed can be utilized for career upward mobility, since they are generally in direct opposition to the positive role model that the protégé needs to emulate. Negative role models can be utilised to view behaviours that the person seeking career progression wants to avoid (Gibson, 2003b).

Role-modelling behaviours materialise in the workplace by people observing their leaders as role models in leadership competencies such as taking initiative, testing skills, and allowing them to learn from experience, which helps them feel much more favourable about their workplace (Kouzes & Posner, 2017). It is further evidenced by research that one of the most effective methodologies for career success that a leader can pass along to their protégé and/or team is the art of role-modelling effective behaviours, and actions. The philosophy is that teams will want to emulate leaders' actions, hence enhancing their own performance, which consequently will lead to career progression (Hader, 2007).

The evolution of role modelling in the workplace has leaders thinking of more effective ways to motivate, lead, and guide their teams. It has secured leaders' belief that role modelling helps them focus on three core skills that enhance retention of team members: inclusion, respect, and fairness (Webb, 2016). This is elaborated in Table 3.2.

Therefore, leaders who model specific behaviours—whether these behaviours are perceived as good behaviours that contribute to the success of the team and organisation or are perceived as negative behaviours that do not support the organisation—will have direct implications on the broader organisation.

The development of individual professionals is often left to their own devices. It is apparent that with formal mentoring programmes for major organisations capped at approximately 10% in the United States (Dobbin & Kalev, 2016), professionals will have to drive their career progression and development. Thus, the few professionals and diverse

Table 3.2 Role model evolution

Solution	Outcome
Inclusion	'Do I belong?'— Staff can become worried if they are going to be excluded from learning-focused projects
Respect	'Do people recognise the value I bring?'— Staff can begin to wonder if their efforts are useful and appreciated
Fairness	'Am I being treated just like everyone else, or do I at least understand the reason that things are the way they are?'— Not ensuring the work environment is a level playing field means that team members can quickly become defensive, which leads to team and organisational dysfunction

Source Webb (2016)

managers in organisations who have the rare opportunity to participate in a formal mentoring programme will benefit greatly from their experiences and organisational sponsorship. However, this statistic leaves 90% of the managerial workforce in the United States, regardless of diversity status, out of the realm to receive formal mentoring. With this in mind, it is incumbent upon those working in these environments to become self-sufficient in the quest for their individual career progression and upward mobility. Furthermore, it is the responsibility of every leader within an organisation that is not participating in a formal mentoring programme to act as a role model to others within the organisation. This is further proven by the persistent underrepresentation of women and minorities (diverse managers and leaders) in C level positions, where the power and influence to support and sponsor mentoring and role-modelling programmes could exist (McDonald & Westphal, 2013).

Role modelling offers all professionals looking to enhance their leadership impact, influence, and career an alternative to the traditionally established mentoring programmes. This is because role modelling offers professionals an opportunity to identify what is relevant to them from the role-modelling experience and what they want to apply in order to meet their career goals informally. One of the most effective methods to learn about expectations is through informal programmes such as role modelling. This objective is to help a less-experienced protégé 'learn the ropes' with respect to what behaviours and communication will be viewed as appropriate and proper. Such exposure helps the protégé avoid career limiting and derailing verbiage, beliefs, and behaviours. This ultimately enhances a positive career outcome for the protégé, as they avoid landmines while enhancing and acquiring necessary competencies and communication styles that are professionally beneficial (Gibson, 2003b; McDonald & Westphal, 2013).

As the conception of what truly depicts talent in organisations—which can be considered to enhance one's career versus what can derail one's career—evolves the necessity for role models and an established framework are even more indispensable. As evidenced in the literature, there continues to be confusion, ambiguity, lack of consistency, and clarity in regards to what encompasses talent that can be directly linked to career progression (Gallardo-Gallardo, Dries, & Gonzalez-Cruz, 2013).

As we think of role-modelling frameworks, we have to consider the impact on gender relations as it relates to career progression outcomes. Data from 200 mentor–protégé programmes show that the biggest impact on career progression comes from male mentors with female protégées (Sosik & Godshalk, 2000). There are several reasons why this gender composition seems to be most effective. Studies indicate that across organisations, male mentors were in higher levels of career development and this lead to their ability to support their protégés more than female mentors, who may hold perceived lesser or lower level positions within an organisation. In addition, there is an overall shortage of female mentors in the context of high-level corporate positions. This supports the reasoning for the execution of role-modelling opportunities within organisations (Sosik & Godshalk, 2000).

However, research does also show that formal mentoring programmes that resulted in both greater career progression for the protégé and enhanced mentor quality are when the mentor and protégé were from the same functional area. This notion is based upon the fact that, perhaps, the mentor can best support and provide guidance to the protégé when the mentor is more knowledgeable in that particular functional area (that is, marketing, finance, or human resources) (Allen et al., 2006). A role model may be selected for not only their role or level within an organisation but also because of their expertise in their functional area. Therefore, if a chief financial officer mentors an individual who is interested in a career in marketing, the results could be less desirable than the chief financial officer mentoring a financial analyst.

Role-modelling behaviour is typically defined with respect to the protégés' reactions to the mentor and well as to the mentor's behaviour (Sosik & Godshalk, 2000). Traditional role-modelling scales have always been comparisons or measurements related to mentoring modelling behaviours (Sosik & Godshalk, 2000). Protégés often engage in 'selective imitation', meaning that they will focus on specific attributes of a particular role model, as opposed to looking at the role model from a global perspective or as all-encompassing (Gibson, 2004). The protégé can be viewed as fairly strategic in determining what specific attributes and behaviours they wish to emulate for career progression.

It is especially important to have the opportunity to determine and emulate positive role-modelling behaviour in early career stages for progression as one continues the pursuit of upward career mobility. Not only does role modelling and mentoring have an impact on career progression, but the by-product of this success also increased compensation (Whitely, Dougherty, & Dreher, 1991).

Unlike mentors, who invariably have a degree of closeness to the protégé based purely on high-touch interaction with mentoring programmes, role models can have both a close and distant relationship with protégés. Close role models have more direct interaction and access to the protégé, in contrast to a distant role model, who is not accessible to protégés. In these cases, the protégé may see this person through video presentations, shareholder meetings, etc.—avenues which do not foster a personal or direct interaction with the protégé (Gibson, 2003b, 2004). These distant role models can be viewed to the protégé as aspirational or similar to how one may view a famous entertainer.

Qualitative Study

The qualitative research study described in this chapter, conducted with management employees from the mid-level to senior level from various organisations in different industries, provides an overview of the various constructs that exist in mentoring and role modelling. This study has implications for continued focus on role modelling and mentorship relationships in organisations for diverse senior and mid-level management leaders, since it (a) determines the desired differences between role modelling and mentoring relationships, (b) provides organisations an opportunity to consider frameworks of both role modelling and mentoring programmes, (c) determines how senior and mid-level management leaders respond to role modelling in contrast to more formal mentoring programmes, and (d) determines the perceived outcomes from role modelling versus mentoring programmes.

Methodology

Diverse senior leaders and middle-management employees were chosen for the study, since generally, mentoring programmes are geared towards this group of contributors. The individuals who were part of this study could participate in two ways: through an anonymous survey and, if they chose to be personally interviewed, they were granted this opportunity by the researcher. About one-third of the respondents volunteered to be personally contacted for an interview. Of the respondents who participated in the interviews were 60% female and 40% male, ranging in age from 35 to 50, and from various industry backgrounds including banking, crisis management, education, and consulting.

The qualitative analysis process involved creating the best way to obtain a feedback from corporate leaders while reserving the opportunity for those who wished to maintain their anonymity. Fifteen qualitative ($n = 15$) surveys were completed by mid-level and senior-level leaders. The mid-level leaders represent those with a minimum of 10 years of experience while the senior-level leaders represent those with a minimum of 20 years of experience. For the purposes of gathering more in-depth information as it relates to role modelling, five in-depth interviews were conducted. Of these five interviewees, 60% are characterised as mid-level leaders and 40% are characterised as senior-level leaders. The survey questions are provided in Appendix 3.1.

Results

Creating categories is a systematic way of grouping themes by common characteristics so that information can be synthesised in an effort to take direct action. Categories can be identified before or after a theme is identified. Based upon the survey and interview data that were collected, 10 categories emerged in the following ranking order: positive/negative behaviour, success, observation, expectations, process, culture/diversity, sponsorship, leadership, communication, and implementation. These categories represent the respondents' most frequent comments and feedback relative to the survey questions on mentoring and role modelling. Definitions of each category are provided in Table 3.3. The detailed survey results are set out in Appendix 3.2.

Table 3.3 Categories listed in the study and definitions of each category

Category	Definition/meaning	Context for study
Positive/negative behaviour	Is the role-modelling behaviour perceived to be negative or positive according to the expectation of corporate behaviour?	For protégés to understand that not all role-modelling behaviour is perceived as positive according to organisational standards
Success	Are there positive career outcomes from mentoring and/or role modelling?	To examine the positive impact of role modelling on overall career trajectory
Observation	Taking note of behaviours of perceived role models	To understand whether observation benefits the protégé
Expectations	What do leaders expect from their protégés and what do protégés expect of leaders?	To help the researcher design a role-modelling framework
Process	What is the process for mentoring and role modelling?	Based on the literature, there needs to be some formalisation of role-modelling processes

(continued)

Table 3.3 (continued)

Category	Definition/meaning	Context for study
Culture/diversity	Are there additional career opportunities for diverse mentees and observers of role modelling?	To answer the question of whether role modelling can offer a broader reach and opportunity for career growth for diverse protégés
Sponsorship	Do the mentors and role-modelling participants, as well as the corporation, endorse and support mentoring?	To understand if there is an opportunity for sponsorship of role modelling and if a framework is established
Leadership	How do organisations support role modelling and mentoring programmes so that they enhance career upward mobility?	Once a framework has been designed, this will provide leaders with a platform to which they can align programmes
Communication	What messaging is given to employees and protégés about mentoring opportunities?	There is an opportunity for role modelling to have formal communication and expectations set forth by leadership
Implementation	What process steps and follow-up criteria are put in place for mentoring programmes to ensure their effectiveness?	Because role-modelling programmes have not established a framework for execution and understanding, respondents focused on mentoring. How can communication be enhanced for both development models?

The researcher noticed that based on respondents' survey results, four of the 10 categories have an explicit expectation of formalisation which directly aligns to mentoring programmes, in contrast to role modelling in the context in which it is being discussed in this chapter. These four categories are process, sponsorship, communication, and implementation. Let us discuss why these are perceived categories for distinguishing between mentoring and role modelling.

Process
Formal mentoring programmes have processes that are designed and implemented for participants. In many cases, leaders within the organisation have previously identified those selected for formal mentoring programmes as high performers. Because role modelling is perceived not to have formal processes, this category specifically addresses formal mentoring programmes.

Sponsorship
Formal mentoring programmes would have garnered sponsorship from not only senior leadership but also from both mentors and mentees. However, for role modelling in the context as discussed here, there would not be an opportunity to solicit sponsorship.

Communication
Formal mentoring programmes generally have a communication plan to align all sponsors and participants. However, role modelling can have informal communication from the context of the individual, that is, the role model is being communicated about by the community of individuals modelling their behaviour.

Implementation
Formal mentoring programmes have an expectation to designate a sense of a beginning and an end as part of an implementation format. Typically, these types of relationships have a start and stop component to them. This way the mentor and mentee know the sunrise and sunset periods of the mentoring relationship. Conversely, with role-modelling programmes, the same formality is not involved and a role-modelling relationship can continue throughout a protégé's entire career.

Analysis of Interviews

Five in-depth interviews were conducted with senior leaders in corporate environments to garner their perspectives on mentoring and role-modelling programmes. Although the identity of the interviewees will remain anonymous, each of them was comfortable with sharing information about the industry which each of them supports. These industries include banking, crisis management, education, and consulting.

Overwhelmingly, findings from the in-depth interviews demonstrated that the interviewees not only understood the concept of role modelling but also supported both role modelling and mentorship in their organisations. As mid-level and senior leaders in their field, they discussed how both role modelling and mentorship have assisted them in elevation in their respected fields. They believe that there is an opportunity to explore both role modelling and mentoring within organisations. However, 100% of the interviewed respondents felt that role modelling was a lower cost, low energy–high impact business practice when it comes to the development of professionals, regardless of where they are in their career trajectory. All of them explained that mentoring programmes must have the approval and involvement of executive leadership while role-modelling programmes can be easily instituted to have an impact at various levels within an organisation. In addition, many of them felt that formal mentoring programmes were contrived and one respondent even described it as a 'dog-and-pony show', meaning that formal mentoring programmes lack authenticity. They are sometimes viewed as a means to an end and a box to check off in order to be elevated to the next level.

The leader from the banking industry stated: 'Role models can be used for the types of inclusion and diversity that an organisation wants to create. Role modelling is about the demonstration of what works in organisations and also promotes representation. It is important that behaviours of those role modelling diverse individuals are thought to have what is considered important to the organisation for upward mobility and success'.

The leader from the crisis management industry stated: 'When leaders in an organisation exhibit positive behaviours these will provide the protégé with positive exposure for the protégé's development. Conversely, if bad or ineffective leadership exists, negative behaviours can be emulated limiting career progression for the protégé'.

The leader from the education sector stated: 'Role modelling is an informal process; if the subject is following a positive and influential role model the results can net into success for the subject. However, one has to access who has influence in an organisation and also if this person is highly regarded from a cultural and performance perspective. This is the only way that role modelling will result in positive outcomes. Otherwise a protégé could be mimicking behaviours that will prove to be detrimental to his/her career'.

The leader from the consulting industry stated: 'There is a tremendous amount of value in having mentors and role models in an organisation. As long as everyone's influence is positive and focused on the right things'.

Discussion

Definitively, the literature relating to career theory supports the necessity of role modelling as a mechanism and tool for career upward mobility and sustainability (Gibson, 2004). However, there is a lack of discipline and consistency around the role-modelling construct. Thus far, a framework designed from qualitative analysis has not been developed for the purposes of role modelling (Gibson, 2004). The purpose of this study was to determine if role modelling, as a less formalised process than mentoring programmes, can have a greater or similar impact, can it prove to be a more cost-effective model for organisations as they look at professional development for their employees and can it reach more participants?

From the findings of both the survey and interviews, it may be concluded that role modelling has a high touch–low structure model. On the other hand, mentoring can have both a high touch–low structure model and a low touch–high structure model, depending on the rules of engagement for the mentoring relationship.

The perceptions of both role modelling and mentoring have a direct impact on how respondents view both methodologies. Role modelling is viewed as the opportunity to observe behaviours that, if emulated, can have a positive impact on career growth. Mentoring is viewed as a more orchestrated process where the selection and inclusion process is much more stringent. Respondents also view role modelling as a more inclusive process that has a broader reach.

Overwhelmingly, respondents felt that the existence of a role-modelling framework leads to sustained career upward mobility. This is further supported by a majority of respondents indicating that role modelling differs from mentoring, with most of the respondents providing detailed explanations of these differences (see Appendix 3.2). This information allows for further research to take place to formalise frameworks and further distinguish role modelling from mentoring programmes and relationships in organisations.

Role-modelling Framework

There are several nuances that one must consider in the development of a role-modelling framework for professionals. The role and impact of role modelling has largely been studied in early career stages, and therefore, research following those individuals aged 40 and over is predominately non-existent. As one progresses in their career and forges a concept and confidence in their abilities and knowledge, the role model's behaviour can begin to be scrutinised by the protégé (Gibson, 2003a, b).

Based on suggestions from survey respondents and literature, there needs to be a formalised role-modelling framework that leaders can consider as they look to role modelling as a professional development tool. As one looks at building the role-modelling framework, one must look at the most important parts of the corporate ecosystem in the role-modelling relationship: protégé, role model and the system (whether known as the organisation, corporation or department). Figure 3.1 shows the interdependencies between these components of the ecosystem.

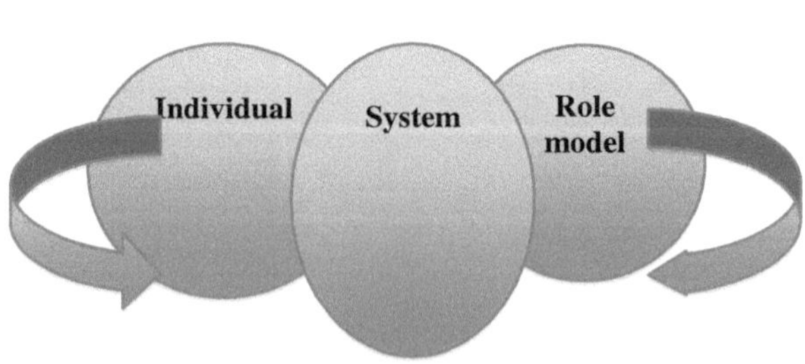

Fig. 3.1 Role-modelling interdependencies

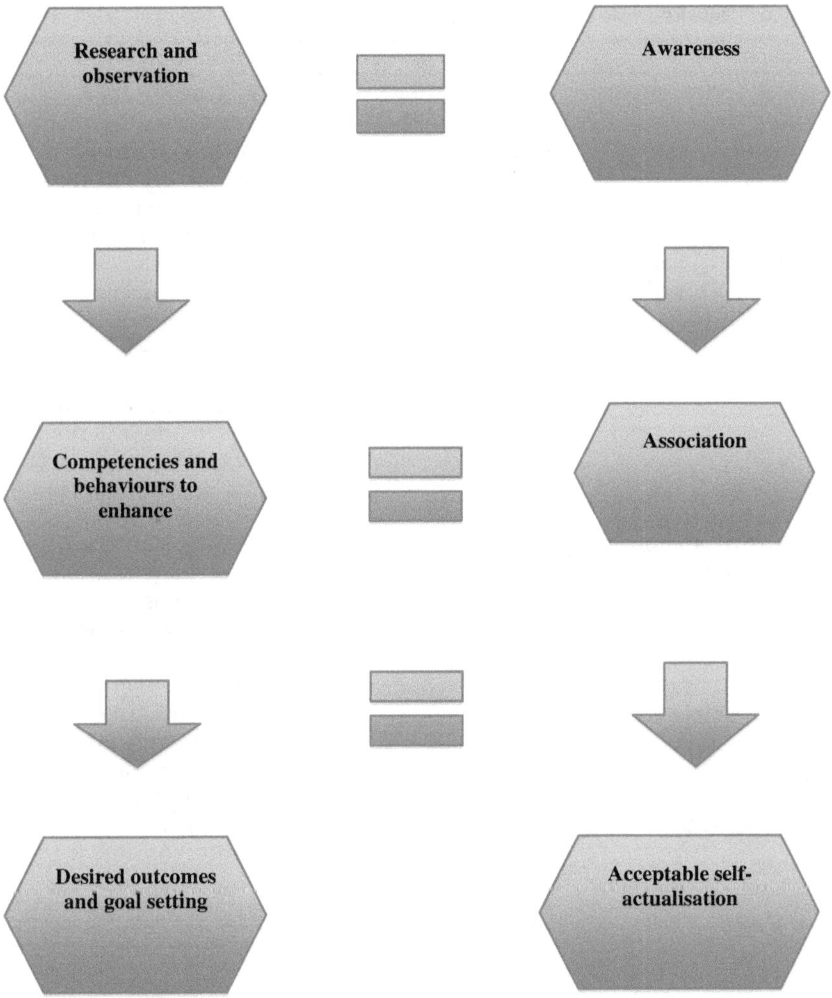

Fig. 3.2 Proposed role-modelling framework

As can be seen in Fig. 3.1, role modelling has external interdependencies, allowing the system to play an important part of the role-modelling relationship, while the individual and role model play equally important roles in forming and maintaining the relationship. Figure 3.2 proposes a role-modelling framework and provides considerations for organisations as they engage in role-modelling initiatives.

Table 3.4 Detailed role-modelling framework

Approach	Outcome	Explanation
Research and observation	Awareness	Once the protégé researches the environment and observes norms, a semblance of what is to be role modelled is realised
Competencies and behaviours to enhance	Association	With knowledge of the competencies and behaviours that the protégé wishes to enhance, association with the appropriate role model will bring about the best results for career progression and enhancement
Desired outcomes and goal setting	Acceptable self-actualisation	It is important for the protégé to put some thought into their desired career trajectory and establish goals in order to maximise outcomes from the role-modelling relationship. This will assist the protégé in having more confidence in the process as well as guide the direction of the relationship

As the literature and survey respondents have communicated, it is clear that a sustainable and easily adaptable role-modelling framework is necessary to assist individuals in navigating the complexity of career succession within corporate environments (Dobbin & Kalev, 2016; Gibson, 2003a, b, 2004). Table 3.4 provides a detailed explanation of the proposed role-modelling framework.

Conclusions

While leaders are constantly challenged with ways in which to maintain their sustainability and long-term solvency, the most impactful strategies focus on people development and talent management. The study in this chapter was designed to distinguish mentoring relationships from role-modelling relationships and had the following additional objectives:

1. Providing organisations with the opportunity to consider frameworks of both role modelling and mentoring programmes.
2. Determining how senior and mid-level management leaders respond to role modelling versus more formal mentoring programmes.
3. Determining the perceived outcomes from role modelling versus mentoring programmes.

In addition, the qualitative analysis provided the researcher with additional insight, which may be summarised as below:

1. A less formalised process such as role modelling can have a greater or similar impact on career growth.
2. Role modelling is a more cost-effective model for professional development, owing to its lack of distinctive structure.
3. Role modelling proves to be a process that reaches more participants.

The qualitative results have demonstrated that career professionals understand that there is a difference between mentoring programmes and role-modelling relationships, but that both can have a positive impact on overall career trajectory. However, the survey of the literature and interviews with respondents indicated that some form of framework needs to be designed to provide a process and proposed outcomes from role modelling. Such a model has been proposed as a result of this study.

An outcome of protégés becoming closer to distant role models is that they typically find negative behaviours and attributes that they find not worth emulating. From a distance, these role models/leaders seem heroic in many respects; however, when closer with a protégé, the heroically viewed role model may have a limited impact on the protégé's individual development (Gibson, 2004).

Considerations for Organisations

Considering that in the United States, only 10% of organisations today have a formal mentoring programme (Dobbin & Kalev, 2016), and 90% of the workforce have no form of organisational sponsorship, role modelling provides an opportunity for organisations to have an impact on a broader and more diverse range of protégés for increased business outcomes and career progression for the protégés.

Role modelling provides organisations with a low-cost alternative to creating, managing, and overseeing formal mentoring programmes. With most major corporations not engaging in mentoring programmes, role modelling provides an avenue by which these organisations can create development opportunities for their team members. Since role modelling can have both close and distant dimensions, it is important to consider that there is a diversity of role models for protégés to emulate. Organisations can provide opportunities for protégés to have both close and distant relationships with role models through creating high-potential programmes, allowing protégés to have skip-level meetings with senior leadership, lunch-and-learn sessions, participate in talent-acquisition initiatives, focus groups, and town hall meetings. Table 3.5 outlines the organisational touch points for role models and outcomes for the protégé.

Ultimately, every protégé is expected to be the catalyst for their individual career development. This means that protégés must understand what behaviours are prevalent and acceptable for career progression within the cultural setting of their organisations, and seek to identify role models that represent these findings. Keeping in mind that most employee populations do not have access to formal mentoring

Table 3.5 Organisational interactions with team members and outcomes

Role model touch points	Dimension: close or distant	Protégé outcomes
High-potential programmes	Close	This provides access to role model, and not only for observation but also to have a greater understanding of behavioural success factors
Skip-level meetings	Close	This allows the protégé one-on-one time with a leader
Lunch-and-learn sessions	Distant	A leader has an opportunity to address specific information about their role within the organisation while answering specific questions from other leaders and protégés
Talent-acquisition initiatives	Close and distant	This can provide the protégé specific insight into behaviours that the functional leader attributes to success. Depending on the protégé's role in the talent-acquisition process, this can be both a close or distant relationship
Focus groups	Close	This allows the protégé time with the leader in a small group setting to discuss a myriad of topics. Further, this close interaction provides the protégé insight into what behaviours, competencies and even strategic initiatives the leader has deemed as important
Town halls	Distant	This provides the leader an opportunity to address a larger group of protégés, but there is typically a larger setting than a focus group

programmes, protégés will have to be vigilant in their quest, identifying and engaging in behaviours that enhance career mobility and sustainability. Role models will not always be the most senior leader or highest ranked in organisation; however, role models will represent to the protégé behaviours that have led to positive outcomes. Nevertheless, it is incumbent upon organisations to ensure that protégés have clear and specific performance measures by which protégés can identify and engage role models. Understanding these variables is an important component for protégés to consider as they engage from a close or distant dimensional perspective with role models.

Future Research

There are several opportunities for future research on role modelling, including to integrate the framework proposed here into active role-modelling relationships to determine its effectiveness, researching the impact of role modelling on professionals over the age of 40 in their careers and if there is any improvement in the upward career mobility of diverse professionals as a result of following the role-modelling framework. In addition, greater focus on specific industries that realise the highest level of outcomes from role-modelling relationships would also be worthwhile. Further, as a continuation of the research presented in this chapter, a longitudinal study with a deeper evaluation from leaders and protégés on the execution of the prescribed role-modelling framework, after considering expectations and outcomes, would be beneficial.

Appendix 3.1

Survey Questions

1. Does a role-modelling framework lead to sustained career positioning or career upward mobility?
2. Does role modelling differ from mentoring?
3. If role modelling differs from mentoring, please briefly describe the differences.
4. Can role modelling and mentoring effectively co-exist in an organisation?
5. Can role modelling enhance the internal talent pool within an organisation?
6. In what ways can role modelling enhance the internal talent pool?
7. Can role modelling shape organisations in the future? If so, in what ways?

8. What is the potential impact of role modelling and breaking the glass ceiling for diverse corporate professionals?
9. How can those involved in role modelling communicate the benefits and impact of role modelling in the workplace, while differentiating it from mentoring?
10. Describe the ways in which you may have benefitted professionally from role modelling and/or mentoring?

Appendix 3.2

Detailed Survey Results and Analysis
There were 15 respondents surveyed. The information below provides an analysis of the results from the survey.

Q1: Does a role-modelling framework lead to sustained career positioning or career upward mobility?

- 87% of respondents stated 'yes'.
- 13% of respondents stated 'no'.

Q2: Does role modelling differ from mentoring?

- 87% of respondents stated 'yes'.
- 13% of respondents stated 'no'.

Q3: If role modelling differs from mentoring, please briefly describe the differences.

- 'Role modelling is a non-active observance and behaviour and mentoring is an activity something both parties are actively engaged in together as a partnership'. (Anonymous survey respondent)
- 'Role modelling = "do what I do" and mentoring = "receive my input and use it as you deem appropriate for you"'. (Anonymous survey respondent)

- 'In order to role model you must work closely with a person so they can see what you're doing. A mentor relationship is less time consuming'. (Anonymous survey respondent)
- 'Role modelling, in my opinion entails more outright behaviours. It focuses more on role model's proficiencies and less on developing those proficiencies in another (mentee). Mentoring, on the other hand requires the mentor to create a value in his/her behaviours. As well as impart those same value added behaviours to another'. (Anonymous survey respondent)
- 'I think mentorship may be more personable than role modelling. Role modelling can serve as an example that people with similar backgrounds can obtain the same success'. (Anonymous survey respondent)

Q4: Can role modelling and mentoring effectively co-exist in an organisation?

- 100% of respondents stated 'yes'.

Q5: Can role modelling enhance the internal talent pool within an organisation?

- 85% of respondents stated 'yes'.
- 13% of respondents stated 'no'.

Q6: In what ways can role modelling enhance the internal talent pool?

- 'If you're looking for someone with a specific skill or behaviour you can design from within by selecting the correct role model for specific candidates'. (Anonymous survey respondent)
- 'Yes, it should equate to a happier company. More free range of speech and ideas. Again, micro-management will

hurt this. It can't be seen as the only means to get promoted'. (Anonymous survey respondent)

- 'Provide examples to others, provide a road map to success or the next level, which many entry-level/mid-level employees seek'. (Anonymous survey respondent)
- 'Role modelling can give the internal talent pool career support to help them achieve their desired goals. It could also allow them to know areas in which to improve their skills. It could give them a clear plan on moving up the ladder'. (Anonymous survey respondent)
- 'If one observes and mimics the behaviour of a successful executive in an organisation you might have the same level of success. Otherwise, you might not ever receive actual face-to-face time with each executive that you admire or that is successful within an organisation'. (Anonymous survey respondent)

Q7: Can role modelling shape organisations in the future? If so, in what ways?

- 'Absolutely. Because you have individuals at all levels observing and modelling the behaviour of those successful in the organisation'. (Anonymous survey respondent)
- 'Yes, in both negative and positive ways. It depends on what is being modelled. I think the behaviour must be defined and the correct candidates selected'. (Anonymous survey respondent)
- 'Yes, the mentor can teach the protégé ways in which they fell short and teach the protégé the ways in which to succeed (perhaps in the way in which the mentor fell short)'. (Anonymous survey respondent)
- 'Role modelling works best in an environment where originality and diversity of thought are not well received'. (Anonymous survey respondent)

- 'It can reshape organisations if they intend on holding on to talented individuals. This can prevent talent drain'. (Anonymous survey respondent)

Q8: What is the potential impact of role modelling and breaking the glass ceiling for diverse corporate professionals?

- 'It has a huge potential impact because it can help to give diverse individuals a fair shot at success and moving up the corporate ladder'. (Anonymous survey respondent)
- 'It can be impactful but only if there has been a lane cleared for diversity and it is at the forefront of leadership within an organisation to make it happen'. (Anonymous survey respondent)
- 'If diverse individuals are selected to be the role model for higher level positions and/or selected to partner with a role model. It would be role modelling in itself'. (Anonymous survey respondent)
- 'Role modelling without sponsorship does very little to break any glass'. (Anonymous survey respondent)
- 'If it creates better communication and teamwork, then it's a win-win'. (Anonymous survey respondent)

Q9: How can those involved in role modelling communicate the benefits and impact of role modelling in the workplace, while differentiating it from mentoring?

- 'I don't think there is a difference. I view the difference as which programme is cookie-cutter corporate to appease management (dog-and-pony show) versus a programme that really helps employees. That banks on corporate implementation'. (Anonymous survey respondent)
- 'Very difficult to do. One advantage is that role modelling can be done in a way that can create a level playing field among employees in an organisation because everyone could be assigned the same person to role model'. (Anonymous survey respondent)

- 'Role modelling is observance from a distance while mentoring is active involvement'. (Anonymous survey respondent)
- 'Role modelling is a way to develop specific behaviour while mentoring suggests what behaviours are favoured and which are not'. (Anonymous survey respondent)
- 'You need to show that role modelling is an actual framework. It is a design that is used for motivation and also leading someone through the process of completing their own desired career goals. Communicate that mentorship is more of an advisory type of relationship'. (Anonymous survey respondent)

Q10: Describe the ways in which you may have benefitted professionally from role modelling and/or mentoring.

- 'I could have had the opportunity to run my plans by a more experienced individual. They could have helped me think about my career choices and my career trajectory in a more logical manner before I made my choices. I think the question that should be asked is why more people who have made it to top positions feel they do not have time to mentor'. (Anonymous survey respondent)
- 'I have had several key roles models during the most formative stages of my career and beyond a shadow of a doubt they had a tremendous impact on me and my career success'. (Anonymous survey respondent)
- 'At my age, I am a mentor but I have no mentors for me. I do have role models and they help me stay consistent with my core values'. (Anonymous survey respondent)
- 'Role modelling helped me set the vision and mentorship helped me with the how'. (Anonymous survey respondent)
- 'Negative, in the two examples I have seen since I have been in my programme, it has only been viewed as a checkmark you have to have in order to get promoted. A gateway to promote those who were going to get promoted anyway. Favourites. Sorry, if this comes across as jaded, but probably the most honest feedback you'll get'. (Anonymous survey respondent)

- 'Role models have assisted in how to express thoughts in a written format or how to perform in a group meeting by looking at others that have done it really well. Role modelling provides a rich playbook to draw upon in certain situations. An effective tool of role modelling is having the ability to pull what was observed out of your toolbox in order to be successful. Whereas, mentoring relationships has been the result of explicit conversations around how they have benefitted early in their career in terms of how to manage or deal with difficult co-workers. The mentor knows the protégé would be seeking advice from real life situations that was discussed and agreed upon ahead of time. This approach has assisted in gleaning better approaches in the workplace that have assisted in managing tough situations'. (Anonymous survey respondent)

Survey Respondents' Comments in Defined Categories

1. Positive/Negative Behaviour
   a. 'Create a more valuable employee'.
   b. 'Yes, in both negative and positive ways. It depends on what is being modelled. I think the behaviour must be defined and the correct candidate selected'.
   c. 'If the role model is ineffective or viewed as unfavourable their behaviour will not be bought into'.
2. Success
   a. 'It helps others see what is possible'.
   b. 'The impact is powerful'.
   c. 'The mentor can teach the protégé ways in which they fell short and teach the protégé the ways in which to succeed (perhaps in the way in which the mentor fell short)'.
3. Observation
   a. 'One can learn about desired behaviours through observations, build an understanding of what great looks like'.

   b. 'You have individuals at all levels observing and modelling the behaviour of those successful in the organisation'.
   c. 'Role modelling is an observance from a distance while mentoring is active involvement'.
4. Expectations
   a. 'Sustained career positioning'.
   b. 'Because it helps others see what is possible'.
   c. 'Suggestions on how to respond, imagine, and next steps to take'.
5. Process
   a. 'Leadership needs to drive and measure role modelling efforts'.
   b. 'If not micro-managed by corporate'.
   c. 'Role modelling needs to be presented as having an actual framework'.
6. Culture/Diversity
   a. 'Corporate support mandatory'.
   b. 'Organisational micro-management should be minimised'.
   c. 'Helps team members envision what is possible'.
7. Sponsorship
   a. 'Role modelling without sponsorship does very little to break any glass'.
   b. 'Create framework for role modelling'.
   c. 'Establish measurements that clearly defines success'.
8. Leadership
   a. 'Leadership sharing stories'.
   b. 'Leadership needs to drive and measure programmes'.
   c. 'Organisations ensure programmes are not cookie cutter'.
9. Communication
   a. 'By being intentional and transparent with communication and goals'.
   b. 'Explain the how while in a role-modelling relationship'.
   c. 'Storytelling'.
10. Implementation
    a. 'Role modelling is an effective way to model behaviour'.
    b. 'Role modelling is a way to develop specific behaviours'.
    c. 'Solid role-modelling framework necessary'.

References

Allen, T., Eby, L., & Lentz, E. (2006). Mentorship behaviours and mentorship quality associated with formal mentoring programs: Closing gap between research and practice. *Journal of Applied Psychology, 91*(3), 567–578.

Dobbin, F., & Kalev, A. (2016). Why diversity programs fail. *Harvard Business Review*, July–August, 52–60. Retrieved on July 27 2017, from https://hbr.org/2016/07/why-diversity-programs-fail.

Gallardo-Gallardo, E., Dries, N., & Gonzalez-Cruz, T. F. (2013). What is the meaning of 'talent' in the world of work? *Human Resource Management Review, 23*(4), 290–300. https://doi.org/10.1016/j.hrmr.2013.05.002.

Gibson, D. (2003a). Developing the professional self-concept: Role model construals in early, middle and late career stages. *Organisation Science, 14*(5), 591–610.

Gibson, D. (2003b). Role models: Reinvigorating a developmental construct in career theory. *Proceedings of the Academy of Management*, Seattle, WA.

Gibson, D. (2004). Role models in career development: New directions for theory and research. *Journal of Vocational Behaviour, 65,* 134–156.

Hader, R. (2007). Follow the leader: Role model peak performance. *Nursing Management, 38*(4), 4–6.

Kouzes, J. M., & Posner, B. Z. (2017). *The leadership challenge: How to make extraordinary things happen in organizations* (6th ed.). Hoboken, NJ: Wiley.

Kram, K., & Isabella, L. (1985). Mentoring alternatives: The role of peer relationships in career development. *Academy of Management Journal, 28*(1), 110–132.

McDonald, M. L., & Westphal, J. D. (2013). Access denied: Low mentoring of women and minority first-time directors and its negative effects on appointments to additional boards. *Academy of Management Journal, 56*(4), 1169–1198.

McDonald, S., Erickson, L. D., & Gatlin, D. (2009). Mentoring in context: A sociological approach to the study of mentoring relationships. In M. I. Keel (Ed.), *Mentoring: Program development, relationships and outcomes* (pp. 21–36). New York: Nova Science Publishers Inc.

Sosik, J. J., & Godshalk, V. M. (2000). The role of gender in mentoring: Implications for diversified and homogenous mentoring relationships. *Journal of Vocational Behaviour, 57*(1), 102–122. https://doi.org/10.1006/jvbe.1999.1734.

Webb, C. (2016). How small shifts in leadership can transform our team dynamic. *McKinsey Quarterly, 2*, 74–81. Retrieved on July 29, 2017, from http://www.mckinsey.com/business-functions/organization/our-insights/how-small-shifts-in-leadership-can-transform-your-team-dynamic.

Whitely, W., Dougherty, T. W., & Dreher, G. F. (1991). Relationship of career mentoring and socioeconomic origin to managers' and professionals' early career progress. *Academy of Management Journal, 34*(2), 331–351.

Section II

Gender and Role Modelling

4

Close and Distant Female Role Models in the Workplace

Alexandra L. Lyman and Stacie F. Chappell

Introduction

The importance of role modelling as a social learning process, although widely accepted, is not well understood (Gibson, 2004; Jung, 1986; Lunenberg, Korthagen, & Swennen, 2007). The belief is that people learn by observing the behaviour of both exemplars of excellence and cases of recovery from failure (Bandura, 1977). However, the disproportionate number of male-to-female leaders, a reality of modern organisations, translates into fewer possibilities for direct relationships with female role models for both men and women. This raises the importance of female role models in the broader social context. This chapter

A. L. Lyman (✉) · S. F. Chappell
Western New England University,
Springfield, MA, USA
e-mail: alexandra.lyman@wne.edu; alyman58@gmail.com

S. F. Chappell
e-mail: stacie.chappell@wne.edu

S. Vidyasagar and P. Hatti (eds.), *Leadership and Role Modelling*,
Palgrave Studies in Leadership and Followership,
https://doi.org/10.1007/978-3-319-69056-8_4

begins with a discussion of role-modelling theory as background to the study. Then the chapter reports on an exploratory study of young adults' perceptions regarding close and distant female role models in the workplace, including how both inform their leadership practice. The study includes both male and female participants and enables comparison of their perspectives. The chapter concludes with a discussion of the findings and recommendations for future practice and research.

Background

A role model is someone that an individual consciously observes and uses to inform their personal or professional identity and behaviour. Three distinctions are important to understanding the complexity of the role model construct: close versus distant role models, positive versus negative role models, and partial versus total role models.

A role model is distinctly different from a mentor because a direct relationship is not necessary for the process (Gibson, 2004). As such, role models can be categorised as close (that is, parents, peers, immediate supervisors, etc.) or distant (that is, business elites, entertainers, celebrities, fictional characters, etc.). Although close role models provide directly observable behaviours, a barrier for identifying direct female role models is the reality of fewer women in leadership positions in the workplace. As such, distant female role models may play an important function. Distant role models provide symbols of possibility, particularly, when there is some element of similarity between the role model and the role model user (that is, gender, race, profession; Chung, 2000; Lockwood & Kunda, 1997). Distant role models are most effective when their domain of excellence (that is, business, sports, etc.) is relevant to the role model user and their level of success seems attainable (Lockwood & Kunda, 1997, 1999). The ubiquity of modern media, particularly in the lives of young people, provides a rich domain for identification with female characters and personalities beyond one's immediate social circle (Hoffner & Buchanan, 2005). Media influence begins from a young age and is significant in how we learn about the world and our place in it (Giles, 2002; Hoffner, 1996). Modern media have unprecedented reach and power. Media messages are carefully crafted to get more hits, views, and ratings. Although these messages may or may not be rooted in reality, they reach us multiple times in our everyday lives and are ultimately important in how we view ourselves, particularly in the context of gender and leadership.

Both close and distant role models can inform the observer of behaviour they wish to emulate or to avoid (Lockwood, Jordan, & Kunda, 2002). A role model may represent the potential best version of the professional's self-concept. However, although individuals may appreciate a role model for their positive traits, they may also reject attributes that they do not wish to acquire or do not fit with their professional style. Gibson, (2003) found positive close role models to be particularly important to young adults in the earlier stages of their career. Alternatively, the choice of positive versus negative role models may relate to the individual's intention to pursue promotion goals or outcome avoidance, respectively (Lockwood et al., 2002).

Finally, observers may identify specific parts of a role model that they wish to emulate (or avoid), or they may identify with the role model in whole. The challenge of the latter for female professionals is obvious given the reality of fewer women than men in managerial roles. Studies suggest there is a sex difference in choosing cross-gender role models and that females tend to be more likely to do so (Javidan, Bemmels, Devine, & Dastmalchian, 1995). However, the partial approach may prove to be more effective in general. Ibarra (1999) found that young professionals who employed the strategy of using total role models were less successful than those who used parts of multiple role models. One study on mid-career managers suggested that role models were important in managerial development, more likely to be a collection of partial role models rather than a single global one, and consisted of both positive and negative learning outcomes (Warhurst, 2011).

There is a need for more research on the phenomenon of role modelling in general (Gibson, 2004; Warhurst, 2011) and specifically the type and influence of female role models on young professionals (Singh, Vinnicombe, & James, 2006). Some evidence suggests that the existence of female role models influences the general view of female leaders and achievement levels of females in particular (Beaman, Duflo,

Pande, & Topalova, 2012). Role model research on young people is often focused on adolescents (that is, 10–18 years of age) and/or on psychosocial factors, as opposed to workplace behaviours (that is, Hurd, Zimmerman, & Xue, 2009; Johnson et al., 2016; Robertson, Blaine, & Cowan, 2005). Studies on the specific influence of role models in workplace and career development are limited. Azmi, Ahmad, Khalique, and Khan (2014) explored the type of role models and career ambitions of adolescent males. Their findings confirmed the relevance of both close and distant role models and the popularity of business, medicine, and engineering aspirations. An exploratory study by Singh et al. (2006), consisting of qualitative interviews with 10 young professional women, reported that participants used a range of partial role models from a variety of domains (that is, gender, close/distant, business/family/arts, etc.). The authors acknowledged the limitation of a small sample size, and the possibility of raised awareness within their sample, before recommending further research with larger samples across genders.

Method

The objective of this exploratory study is to contribute to a better understanding of the influence of female role models on young adults in the early stage of their career development. Who are the close and distant female role models? What specific traits do young adults notice? Finally, what meaningful lessons do role model users hope to emulate, or avoid, as they develop their careers and workplace identities?

Ethics approval was obtained for this study from the Western New England University Ethics Review Board. Phenomenology underpinned the research objective of better understanding the influence of female role models in the workplace. A qualitative open-ended questionnaire was employed to gather the data. The questionnaire was revised after an initial beta-test to better enquire into the emergent theme of close versus distant role models (Fig. 4.1).

The participants initially responded to the three questions without any prompting. Then participants were asked to reflect on the identified female role model to clarify whether it was someone they knew directly

1. Thinking about your current and future career, who do you personally consider to be a female role model?

Role models serve a vital function by helping us create, experiment with, and define our self-concept. By paying attention to a role model's style, traits, and skills, we develop our own.

2. What traits does she have that make her a role model?

3. What does she teach you about the workplace?

Fig. 4.1 Open-ended questionnaire

or whether it was someone they were familiar with from the broader media. We then asked them to answer the same questions for the group they did not mention the first time around (that is, if they chose someone they knew personally, they were to answer the questions with someone from the broader media mind and vice versa).

Setting and Sample

The study population consisted of undergraduate students in the College of Business at Western New England University. The original sample of 71 students was collected from six different classes during a two-week period in October 2016. The age of participants in the original sample ranged from 17 to 48 years. Given that the focus of this study was on the perceptions of young adults, the three participants more than 30 years of age were deleted from the sample. The age of participants in the final sample ranged from 17 to 28 years with a mean age of 20 years. Students were invited to participate in this optional activity and did not receive any credit for doing so. The researchers were given time at the beginning or end of each class to introduce the research and administer the survey.

Data Analysis

Data from the surveys were transcribed and independently content analysed by both researchers. Emergent themes for each question were identified and synthesised for the domain, related, and lessons learned from the role models identified by participants. Where respondents mentioned more than one trait or lesson learned, these were coded separately. Themes were ranked according to their frequency within the responses overall and for the male and female subsets in the data.

Results

We reflect on the survey results by reporting on themes for each of the three questions asked: categories of role models identified by participants, the traits participants valued in the identified role models, and finally, the lessons participants felt they learned from the identified role models. We identify similarities and differences in male versus female respondents and use illustrative participant quotes where relevant to further illuminate the data.

Categories of Role Models

Close Role Models

Close female role models identified by participants can be classified into four broad categories: members of their family (mother, sister, grandmother), colleagues from their work environment, school professionals, and friends (Table 4.1).

The predominance of mothers as a role model for both male and female participants is notable. Three categories were tied for the next most common response: female colleagues, school professionals, and theoretical figures. Female colleagues included specific names of people who occupied roles ranging from the direct manager of the respondent to the CEO. Five participants responded by describing a theoretical figure rather than a specific person:

Table 4.1 Categories of close female role models

Category	Total	Female	Male
Mother	32	17	15
Female colleague at work	5	1	4
None	6	1	5
School professional	5	3	2
Theoretical figure	5	1	4
Sister	4	2	2
Friend/girlfriend	4	2	2
Celebrity	4	2	2
Grandmother	3	1	2

Someone who isn't afraid to stand up to strong male personalities (female).

I see a female role model as very stern and strict but at the same time caring and understanding (male).

I think role models share many of same qualities regardless of gender. Gender should not be a factor in the role model (male).

Someone who has extreme success and shows a great deal of leadership (male).

Despite specific instructions to choose a close role model, some participants named well-known figures they were unlikely to know personally (that is, Kerri Walsh-Jennings, Michelle Obama, Ellen DeGeneres, Meredith Marakovits, and Oprah Winfrey). Six participants (one female and five male) did not identify a close female role model although they did identify a distant female role model.

Distant Role Models

Distant female role models identified by participants represent a broader range of categories including individuals from popular culture (that is, actresses, comedians, singers, and celebrities), athletes, political figures, journalists, businesswomen, or fictional characters from television (Table 4.2).

Table 4.2 Categories of distant female role models

Category	Total	Female	Male
None	18	2	16
Athlete	11	3	8
Political figure	7	3	4
Singer	6	5	1
Celebrity	6	3	3
Actress	5	5	0
Fictional character	5	3	2
Theoretical figure	4	2	2
Comedian	3	3	0
Businesswoman	2	0	2
Journalist	1	1	0

The largest category consists of the 18 participants who did not identify a distant female role model. This category represents almost a third of all participants in the study and well over a third of the male respondents. All these respondents did specify a close female role model. However, this category of 18 responses included four of the five participants who described a theoretical figure rather than a specific individual as a close female role model, referred to above.

The next most common category of distant female role model was that of an athlete (Alex Morgan, Helen Maroulis, Jennie Finch, Katie Nolan, Serena Williams, Stacey Lewis, and Jen Welter). Other significant categories included actresses/comedians (Amy Schumer, Audrey Hepburn, Ellen DeGeneres, Emma Watson, Julia Roberts, Radio Amy, and Viola Davis), political figures (Michelle Obama and Hillary Clinton), and singers (Taylor Swift, Christina Grimmie, Miley Cyrus, and Reba McEntire). More male respondents identified athletes as distant role models than women. Male respondents did not identify actresses, comedians, or journalists. Female respondents were more likely to mention a distant role model in the entertainment industry. The majority of participants identified a real person as a distant female role model, although five chose a fictional character from a popular television series. A small list of names was identified by both male and female respondents that included Alex Morgan, Hillary Clinton, Michelle Obama, Oprah Winfrey, and Taylor Swift (Table 4.3).

Table 4.3 Distant female role models—real and fictional characters

	Real people	Fictional characters
Male	Alex Morgan (2), Helen Maroulis (2), Hillary Clinton (2), Ivanka Trump, Jen Welter, Kim Cody ASCM, Mia Hamm, Michelle Obama (2), Oprah Winfrey (3), Serena Williams, Stacey Lewis, Taylor Swift	Marie from Everybody Loves Raymond, Michonne from The Walking Dead
Female	Alex Morgan, Amy Schumer, Audrey Hepburn, Ellen DeGeneres (2), Emma Watson (3), Hillary Clinton, Christina Grimmie, Jennie Finch, Julia Roberts, Katie Couric, Katie Nolan, Khloe Kardashian, Michelle Obama (2), Miley Cyrus, Oprah Winfrey, Radio Amy, Reba McIntyre, Taylor Swift (2), Viola Davis	Leslie Knope from Parks and Recreation, Meredith Grey from Grey's Anatomy, and Olivia Pope from How to Get Away with Murder

Traits of Role Models

Traits of Close Role Models

Traits describing close female role models were coded into 16 thematic categories (Table 4.4). In order of overall frequency, starting with the most commonly mentioned, they are as follows: caring (1), hard-working (2), determined (3), knowledgeable (4), strong (4), independent (5), responsible (5), motivated (5), confident (6), friendly (6), values-based (7), leader (8), recognised/connected (8), inspiring (8), teacher (9), and optimistic (9).

The traits of *caring* and *hard-working* were the most frequently mentioned, and therefore ranked first and second, respectively, by both female and male respondents. Female respondents referenced the trait of

Table 4.4 Traits of close female role models

Trait	Overall most commonly mentioned (# responses)	Female order of most commonly mentioned (# responses)	Male order of most commonly mentioned (# responses)
Caring	1	1 (24)	1 (20)
Hard-working	2	2 (16)	2 (15)
Determined	3	3 (15)	5 (5)
Knowledgeable	4	8 (5)	3 (9)
Strong		5 (8)	4 (6)
Independent		7 (6)	5 (5)
Responsible	5	6 (7)	6 (4)
Motivated		4 (9)	7 (2)
Confident	6	8 (5)	6 (4)
Friendly		8 (5)	6 (4)
Values-based	7	10 (3)	4 (6)
Leader		9 (3)	6 (4)
Recognised/ connected	8	8 (5)	7 (2)
Inspiring		7 (6)	8 (1)
Teacher	9	9 (3)	7 (2)
Optimistic		8 (5)	N/A (0)

determination almost as frequently as *hard-working* and three times more frequently than male respondents. Female respondents also mentioned the trait of *motivated* more often than male respondents. Male respondents mentioned the traits of *knowledgeable*, *values-based*, and *leader* more often. Finally, *optimistic* was only mentioned by female respondents.

Traits of Distant Role Models

The traits describing distant female role models were coded into 27 thematic categories (Table 4.5). In order of overall frequency, they are listed as follows: strong (1), determined (2), caring (2), independent (3), truthful/authentic (4), feminist/pioneering (5), confident/proud (5), beneficent (6), motivated (6), hard-working (6), talented (7), respectful (7), powerful (7), optimistic (8), successful (8), courageous/brave (8), intelligent (9), friendly (9), business skills (9), inspirational (10),

Table 4.5 Traits of distant female role models

Trait	Overall most commonly mentioned (# responses)	Female order of most commonly mentioned (# responses)	Male order of most commonly mentioned (# responses)
Strong	1	1 (9)	4 (3)
Determined	2	3 (7)	3 (4)
Caring		4 (6)	2 (5)
Independent	3	2 (8)	5 (2)
Truthful/authentic	4	4 (6)	4 (3)
Feminist/pioneer	5	8 (2)	1 (6)
Confident/proud		6 (4)	3 (4)
Beneficent		5 (5)	6 (1)
Motivated	6	7 (3)	4 (3)
Hard-working		8 (2)	3 (4)
Talented		7 (3)	5 (2)
Respectful	7	7 (3)	5 (2)
Powerful		7 (3)	5 (2)
Optimistic		6 (4)	N/A
Successful	8	9 (1)	4 (3)
Courageous/brave		9 (1)	4 (3)
Intelligent		7 (3)	N/A (0)
Friendly	9	8 (2)	6 (1)
Business skills		9 (1)	5 (2)
Inspirational		8 (2)	N/A (0)
Problem solver		8 (2)	N/A (0)
Ethical		8 (2)	N/A (0)
Leader	10	9 (1)	6 (1)
Reliable		9 (1)	6 (1)
Loyal		9 (1)	6 (1)
Appearance		N/A (0)	6 (2)
Open-minded	11	9 (1)	N/A (0)

problem solver (10), values-based (10), leader (10), reliable (10), loyal (10), appearance (10), and open-minded (11).

The four most commonly cited traits were *strong*, *determined*, *caring*, and *independent*. Female respondents provided almost twice as many traits as male respondents to describe distant role models. They most frequently described distant role models as *strong*, *independent*, *determined*, and *truthful/authentic*. The most frequent theme for male respondents was that of *feminist/pioneer*.

Lessons from Role Models

Lessons from Close Role Models

The lessons learned from close female role models were coded into nine thematic categories (Table 4.6). In order of overall frequency, they are as follows: hard work is necessary for success (1), woman in the workplace (2), advice for how to act in the workplace (3), do your best (4), speak your truth and hold to your values (4), work–life balance is possible (5), keep your eye on the bigger picture (5), be patient and friendly (6), and embrace diversity (6).

The most common lesson, cited by an equal number of female and male respondents, related to the importance of hard work and not giving up, as illustrated by the following quotes:

Table 4.6 Themes in lessons learned from close female role models

Lesson learned	Overall most commonly mentioned (# responses)	Female order of most commonly mentioned (# responses)	Male order of most commonly mentioned (# responses)
Hard work is necessary for success	1 (18)	1 (9)	1 (9)
Woman in the workplace	2 (10)	2 (6)	3 (4)
Advice for how to act in the workplace	3 (8)	4 (3)	2 (5)
Do your best	4 (5)	5 (2)	4 (3)
Speak your truth and hold to your values	4 (5)	3 (4)	6 (1)
Work–life balance is possible	5 (4)	5 (2)	5 (2)
Keep your eye on the bigger picture	5 (4)	4 (3)	6 (1)
Be patient and friendly	6 (3)	N/A (0)	4 (3)
Embrace diversity	6 (3)	6 (1)	5 (2)

She teaches me how to be hardworking and to never give up, even when things are difficult (female).

That if you work hard and don't give up, you will be successful in life (male).

She teaches me that if you work hard, you can do anything you set your mind to. Not many bosses are female so I am very inspired by her (female).

The next most frequent theme in the lessons learned from role models related specifically to the role of women in the workplace. For some respondents, their role model was an exemplar of equal opportunity for women:

Women can thrive even in a male dominated industry (female).

I'm not a woman, but she taught me that women can succeed just as well as men (male).

Women can do just as much and have just as loud a voice (female).

That education, expertise, interpersonal skills, and experience will always prevail, regardless of any other bias (male).

In contrast, some respondents described lessons they learned that illustrated an awareness of challenges that still exist for women in the workplace:

Women work very hard and are not always appreciated for their efforts by their male and even female bosses (male).

Woman should be treated as equals in terms of pay and opportunity for growth (female).

The workplace is tough for women, often have to be twice as qualified and work twice as hard to be seen as doing the job effectively (male).

The third theme related to lessons learned regarding how to act in the workplace, in particular, the importance of professionalism:

The workplace is a place of professionalism a second home (respect it) (female).

> *How to conduct myself, make connections, how I should work* (male).
>
> *To hold myself to high standards by always remaining professional* (female).

The importance of doing your best at work was again represented by both male and female respondents:

> *Hold your own and strive to be the best. Don't let others dictate what you are capable of* (female).
>
> *Always put my best effort into anything I do. Always push harder for better* (male).

In contrast, more female respondents described a lesson regarding speaking their truth and giving voice to their values:

> *She teaches me to hold my ground, always stand for what I believe in, and always speak my mind where appropriate* (female).
>
> *To always say what you feel is important, even if your job isn't considered important* (female).
>
> *To be myself and stand up for what I believe in and my values* (male).

Although equally represented by both male and female respondents, the work–life balance category contained two sub-themes that fell along gender lines. Female responses spoke to the fact that '[t]here can be work-life balance'. Male responses described how their role model had taught them 'to work smart, not hard'.

More female responses were coded as *keeping your eye on the bigger picture*:

> *Helping people out even when you have nothing to gain is worth it in the end. You never know who they know or what they can make happen for you* (female).
>
> *It is important to stay professional, but look beyond just the job you are assigned to, rather look at the big picture and always look to be continuously improving in your career* (female).

Only male respondents described lessons regarding the importance of being friendly to your co-workers including the advice to 'make sure your boss is your friend'. Both female and male respondents described lessons relating to the importance of 'embracing diversity' (male) including 'how to deal with people who may not have similar thoughts as you' (female).

Lessons from Distant Role Models

The lessons learned from distant female role models were coded into eight thematic categories (Table 4.7). In order of overall frequency, they are listed as follows: women can succeed as well as men (1), hard work is necessary for success (2), respect others/be kind (3), the responsibility of leadership (3), be tenacious in the face of adversity (4), hold to your values (4), connections are important (5), and love what you do (5).

Table 4.7 Themes in lessons learned from distant female role models

Lesson learned	Overall most commonly mentioned (# responses)	Female order of most commonly mentioned (# responses)	Male order of most commonly mentioned (# responses)
Women can succeed as well as men	1 (14)	1 (8)	1 (6)
Hard work is necessary for success	2 (7)	2 (4)	2 (3)
Respect others/ be kind	3 (5)	3 (3)	3 (2)
The responsibility of leadership	3 (5)	3 (3)	3 (2)
Be tenacious in the face of adversity	4 (4)	4 (2)	3 (2)
Hold to your values	4 (4)	4 (2)	3 (2)
Connections are important	5 (3)	5 (1)	3 (2)
Love what you do	5 (3)	3 (3)	N/A

The most common theme overall, and for both female and male respondents, was that women can succeed as well as men:

> *Being a woman doesn't hold you back, women can do everything a man can do* (female).
>
> *Women can find success in highly aggressive and physical sports. Just as strong and athletic as men* (male).
>
> *Women can make it in the corporate world with hard work and knowledge* (female).
>
> *She is teaching us all that the world is changing and maybe it is time for a woman president* (male).

The next most frequently cited lesson learned from distant role models reinforced the necessity 'to work hard to achieve your dreams' (male). An equal number of male and female respondents spoke about the 'possibilities and opportunities available with hard work' (female).

The next most common lesson is a variation in the theme of kindness mentioned above. However, the nuance here is being respectful towards others:

> *Being truthful and respectful are necessities* (female).
>
> *Respect the views of others, every idea can have value* (male).

The responsibility of leadership was a new theme that emerged in relation to distant role models. The participants learned the significance of 'doing good for others' (female), the notion that as a leader 'you represent more than yourself' (male), and the importance of 'involvement in the community' (male).

The respondents believe that distant role models taught them the lesson of having tenacity in the face of adversity:

> *No matter how much life tries to get you down, you can always get back up and keep going* (female).
>
> *Nothing can keep you down* (male).

The final three themes in the lessons learned from distant role models, although small in the frequency of responses, each had high fidelity in their meaning. First, the importance of connections is evident in the statement that 'colleagues can be useful resources' (male) and the advice to 'network as much as you can because you never know who you will meet' (male). Second, the theme of holding to your values is reflected in the reminders to 'use your voice and be an individual' (female) and to not 'be afraid to stand out on what you believe' (male). Finally, female respondents identified the lesson that 'loving your job is crucial' (female).

Discussion of Results

Within the data, there were several overarching themes that were incorporated into responses for both close and distant role models.

Type of Role Model

Findings from this study suggest that both close and distant role models are important to young adults. Close role models chosen by the respondents were mostly family members, between mothers, grandmothers, and sisters, which speaks to the continuing importance and influence of family in the early career stage (Giles, 2002; Hoffner, 1996).

Several male respondents declined to suggest a close role model and instead listed traits the desired role model would possess. Similarly, 21 of 24 'no response' for a distant role model were from males, suggesting difficulty in relating to cross-gender distant role models, a finding that is consistent with previous research (Avolio, Zhu, Koh, & Bhati, 2004; Gibson, 2004). It may be that respondents were not able to select someone on the spot, or that they do not identify with a distant female role model at all. It may be that male role models more easily come to mind because they are more prominent, or because there is a lack of strong female role models.

The presence of sports figures as distant female role models in the findings is encouraging given their potential to promote empowerment and gender equity (Meier, 2015). More men identified a sports figure, which suggests perhaps a larger interest in sports (Carter, 2013). Women generally have to be exceptional to be noted, and most of the female athletes mentioned are extremely well known and prominent in their sports, in some cases more of a brand than a person (Eagly, Karau, & Makhijani, 1995). More women chose role models in the entertainment arena, which raises questions related to the over-sexualisation of our musicians and movie stars, and the pressure put on young women to emulate their famous counterparts (Hoffner, 1996; Hoffner & Buchanan, 2005).

Also interesting is that during the time that this study was conducted, the US Presidential Election was in progress. Prominent women such as First Lady Michelle Obama and presidential candidate Hillary Clinton, while mentioned, were not as widely chosen as we would have expected. Consistent with studies, younger individuals tend to choose distant role models that they aspire to be like, and whether they voted for Hillary or not, they perhaps do not aspire to be like her, either due to the leadership double bind or the course taken by election rhetoric.

Also noteworthy was that most of the distant role models were real women rather than a fictional character. This suggests that it is easier to identify with, admire, and relate to a real person than it is to accept role modelling from a fictional character (Ashforth, Schinoff, & Rogers, 2016).

However, a few respondents also chose role models in sports and entertainment, despite instructions to list a role model they actually know. This indicates that perhaps those distant role models feel close because a respondent may feel they can relate to or has a personal connection to the role model and what they represent through personal or wishful identification (Giles, 2002; Hoffner, 1996; Hoffner & Buchanan, 2005). In this case, the individual is basing their identification on what they have seen or heard secondhand from the target. The individual must then fill in the gaps themselves, often with their imagination. The identification, to some extent, is not real or realistic, but rather what the individual is seeking in a target (Ashforth et al., 2016).

Traits of Role Models

It is interesting that the traits used to describe both close and distant role models were all positive. Some of these traits are typically expected of women, such as motherly, nurturing, sweet, friendly, and giving (Costa, Terracciano, & McCrae, 2001). Interestingly, a small number of male respondents mentioned being patient and friendly; however, these were not on the list for female respondents. Although some stereotypes of women were prevalent, these are not inherently negative in and of themselves. However, defining a woman by her motherly and kind nature can be damaging to female progression in the workplace due to stereotype threat (Cheryan, Plaut, Davies, & Steele, 2009; Davies, Spencer, & Steele, 2005).

Other traits described a modern vision of women in the workplace such as strong, hard-working, determined, confident, independent, powerful, and inspiring (Beaman et al., 2012; Staw, 2004). These results are encouraging evidence of feminism's impact in promoting assertive and confident behaviours and addressing gender inequality (Saunders, 2016). Such juxtaposition of feminine and masculine traits raises the issue of the leadership double bind and the standard to which women are generally held (Cheryan et al., 2009; Davies et al., 2005).

Close female role models were also described as smart, ethical, and as capable of leading. These findings point to elements of transformational leadership, such as utilising intellectual stimulation and recognition of values to help individuals achieve personal and professional growth (Avolio et al., 2004).

Some gender differences existed in the traits identified by participants. Most notable is the large number of female respondents that named the trait of determination for close role models. This quality may not be as recognisable to men, who do not often see that women have to work twice as hard to achieve what their male peers have (Eagly et al., 1995).

Only female respondents identified the trait of optimistic for both close and distant role models. We cannot know whether this is a product of improvements in the workplace for women, or the need to be optimistic to negate continued stereotype threat. The connection between optimism and transformational leadership is worth noting, as transformational leaders actively keep morale high, and inspire and help individuals plan for and reach future goals (Avolio et al., 2004).

In addition, female respondents provided almost twice as many traits to describe their distant role model, indicating that they are more directly influenced by these women than the male respondents were, based on their ability to offer specific traits in greater quantity. Only male respondents mentioned appearance. The female respondents did not use outward looks as a basis for identifying traits that made a role model, a role model indicating that looks are not a priority when identifying useful distant role models. Although this does not represent a large amount of males, it does raise questions around cross-gender identification (Gibson, 2004).

Male respondents largely mention traits that identified a role model that was the first woman to do something, or contributed to the advancement of women in some way. This is an easy way to recognise a woman as accomplished in her field, and as a role model for others, as that is how many women gain notoriety. However, these traits are not specific to how the role model accomplished goals in the workplace. Our male respondents did not mention several traits that were prominent with female respondents, which includes optimistic, intelligent, ethical, inspirational, problem solver, and open-minded. This points to the idea that perhaps women in media are too distant to be relatable, at least to the male population. Men can identify these traits in the women they know on a personal level, but struggle to assign the same attributes to a distant female role model in media, because they have not experienced firsthand that these women possess such traits, making the role model's impact low (Avolio et al., 2004; Gibson, 2004).

Lessons Learned

Consistent with the positive traits described above, the lessons learned from both close and distant role models were largely inspiring and empowering. Clearly, participants had identified positive target role models that they aspired to emulate (Gibson, 2003). Being told that women can do it all, to stand up for yourself and your beliefs, and follow your dreams are important messages (Beaman et al., 2012). This supports Gibson's (2003) findings that positive role models are important to young adults and that female role models are particularly important for the professional development of women in the face of negative stereotypes and discrimination (Lockwood, 2006).

Lessons learned from both close and distant role models centred around hard work, voicing your values, and knowing how to act in the workplace. These themes that have come up both in traits and lessons learned from distant role models have clearly resonated with respondents. This further supports the assertion that young adults will adopt partial emulation of different role models and later adapt them to their own personal workplace to gauge their effectiveness (Avolio et al., 2004; Gibson, 2003).

An interesting lesson from distant role models was that women can do anything a man can do—however, more women noted this than men did. Male respondents were more likely to mention networking and making connections (actions typically associated with males) as being important to success. Both male and female respondents acknowledged that women still face challenges in the workplace that impede their career progress and overall success (Eagly et al., 1995). This suggests that both male and female respondents have witnessed, heard about, or potentially experienced similar challenges. Another universal theme was the idea that hard work is the key to success. This suggests that female participants in this study believe they will be given a fair shot to succeed in the workplace, despite potential discrimination, thus mediating stereotype threat (Davies et al., 2005).

Female respondents frequently mentioned that they learned to speak up for themselves and stand up for what they believe in. Essentially, they learned from close personal role models to use their voice, even when, at times, they may not feel they have a voice. Women, as a disadvantaged group, have not always traditionally been given a seat at the table, or have had their opinions taken seriously. But women who fight policies and traditions that previously kept females out of power or industry make it easier for other women to enter masculine domains and become a role model for future women (Beaman et al., 2012).

This gives other women the confidence and support (as a result of impactful feminism) to stand up for themselves and their beliefs (Saunders, 2016). Learning how to effectively use your voice is an important skill in the workplace.

Conclusion

In this exploratory study, we sought to contribute to the understanding of close and distant female role models in the workplace. The results concur with other studies that mothers remain important as female role models to late adolescents at the beginning stages of their career. Participants were able to identify and describe a range of close and distant female role models with a range of traditionally masculine and feminine traits. This study contributes to understanding gender similarities and differences in perceptions of female role models. Female respondents identified the trait of determination more frequently than male respondents. Additionally, more females than males identify with distant female role models, many of whom are portrayed at the pinnacle of success. This suggests the role that media portrayals of women are critical and perhaps more salient to females.

As an exploratory study, there are a number of limitations worth mentioning. The single site of data collection and the relatively small sample size are noted. Further studies might explore multiple collection sites and larger samples to determine whether the themes identified in this study are related to demographics of the sample employed. Furthermore, a longitudinal study would identify trends in attitudes and opinions. The methodology employed open-ended written responses, which precluded probing further into responses. Future research might employ the use of focus groups to enable deeper exploration of meaning. Despite these limitations, the results from this initial study do support a number of broad implications for practice, both in the workplace and in educational settings.

These findings procured from undergraduate students, offer insight into how businesses may encourage and facilitate impactful role modelling in the workplace, particularly for new hires and young professionals.

When a new hire is on-boarded, supervisors can initiate a conversation about role models. Recognising the importance of mothers for this group, asking a new hire about what their mother taught them about being successful in the workplace will reveal critical information about what this individual values and what they are looking for in a role model.

Managers can also share examples of their own close and distant role models with direct reports with the dual intention of educating them about potential close role models in the organisation and stimulating their thinking about how distant role models can be useful. They can also ask direct reports about their current close and distant role models. It is important to remain open to the fact that these role models will come from a variety of places and may not include the manager.

Finally, to maintain communication, managers should build into developmental conversations (that is, when conducting performance reviews, goal setting, or allocating new assignments) the opportunity to explore both close and distant role models, what has been beneficial, and what is lacking in the individual's current role model(s).

Finally, given the lack of female role models identified from workplace settings, a recommendation for practice is greater attention to and use of female role models in the curriculum of university business programmes.

References

Ashforth, B. E., Schinoff, B. S., & Rogers, K. M. (2016). 'I identify with her', 'I identify with him': Unpacking the dynamics of personal identification in organizations. *Academy of Management Review, 41*(1), 28–60.

Avolio, B. J., Zhu, W., Koh, W., & Bhatia, P. (2004). Transformational leadership and organizational commitment: Mediating role of psychological empowerment and moderating role of structural distance. *Journal of Organizational Behavior, 25*(8), 951–968.

Azmi, S. A., Ahmad, A., Khalique, N., & Khan, Z. (2014). Role models and occupational ambitions of in-school male adolescents. *Industrial Psychiatry Journal, 23*(1), 36–39.

Bandura, A. (1977). *Social learning theory*. Englewood Cliffs, NJ: Prentice-Hall.

Beaman, L., Duflo, E., Pande, R., & Topalova, P. (2012). Female leadership raises aspirations and educational attainment for girls: A policy experiment in India. *Science, 335*(6068), 582–586. https://doi.org/10.1126/science.1212382.

Carter, B. (2013, December 17). ABC viewers tilt female for a network light on sports. *The New York Times*. Retrieved on 2 April 2016 from http://www.nytimes.com/2013/12/18/business/media/abc-viewers-tilt-female-for-a-network-light-on-sports.html?_r=0.

Cheryan, S., Plaut, V. C., Davies, P. G., & Steele, C. M. (2009). Ambient belonging: How stereotypical cues impact gender participation in computer science. *Journal of Personality and Social Psychology, 97*(6), 1045–1060.

Chung, K. S. (2000). Role models and arguments for affirmative action. *The American Economic Review, 90*(3), 640–648.

Costa, P. T., Jr., Terracciano, A., & McCrae, R. R. (2001). Gender differences in personality traits across cultures: Robust and surprising findings. *Journal of Personality and Social Psychology, 81*, 322–331.

Davies, P. G., Spencer, S. J., & Steele, C. M. (2005). Clearing the air: Identity safety moderates the effects of stereotype threat on women's leadership aspirations. *Journal of Personality and Social Psychology, 88*(2), 276–287.

Eagly, A. H., Karau, S. J., & Makhijani, M. G. (1995). Gender and the effectiveness of leaders: A meta-analysis. *Psychological Bulletin, 117*(1), 125–144.

Gibson, D. E. (2003). Developing the professional self-concept: Role model construals in early, middle, and late career stages. *Organization Science, 14*(5), 591–610.

Gibson, D. E. (2004). Role models in career development: New directions for theory and research. *Journal of Vocational Behavior, 65*(1), 134–156.

Giles, D. C. (2002). Parasocial interaction: A review of the literature and a model for future research. *Media Psychology, 4*(3), 279–304.

Hoffner, C. (1996). Children's wishful identification and parasocial interaction with favorite television characters. *Journal of Broadcasting & Electronic Media, 40*(3), 389–402.

Hoffner, C., & Buchanan, M. (2005). Young adults' wishful identification with television characters: The role of perceived similarity and character attributes. *Media Psychology, 7*(4), 325–351.

Hurd, N. M., Zimmerman, M. A., & Xue, Y. (2009). Negative adult influences and the protective effects of role models: A study with urban adolescents. *Journal of Youth and Adolescence, 38*(6), 777–789.
Ibarra, H. (1999). Provisional selves: Experimenting with image and identity in professional adaptation. *Administrative Science Quarterly, 44*(4), 764–791.
Javidan, M., Bemmels, B., Devine, K. S., & Dastmalchian, A. (1995). Superior and subordinate gender and the acceptance of superiors as role models. *Human Relations, 48*(11), 1271–1284.
Johnson, S. K., Buckingham, M. H., Morris, S. L., Suzuki, S., Weiner, M. B., Hershberg, R. M., et al. (2016). Adolescents' character role models: Exploring who young people look up to as examples of how to be a good person. *Research in Human Development, 13*(2), 126–141.
Jung, J. (1986). How useful is the concept of 'role model?' A critical analysis. *Journal of Social Behavior and Personality, 1*(4), 524.
Lockwood, P. (2006). Someone like me can be successful: Do college students need same-gender role models? *Psychology of Women Quarterly, 30*(1), 36–46.
Lockwood, P., Jordan, C., & Kunda, Z. (2002). Motivation by positive or negative role models: Regulatory focus determines who will best inspire us. *Journal of Personality and Social Psychology, 83*(4), 854–864.
Lockwood, P., & Kunda, Z. (1997). Superstars and me: Predicting the impact of role models on the self. *Journal of Personality and Social Psychology, 73*(1), 91–103.
Lockwood, P., & Kunda, Z. (1999). Increasing the salience of one's best selves can undermine inspiration by outstanding role models. *Journal of Personality and Social Psychology, 76*(2), 214–228.
Lunenberg, M., Korthagen, F., & Swennen, A. (2007). The teacher educator as a role model. *Teaching and Teacher Education, 23*(5), 586–601.
Meier, M. (2015). The value of female sporting role models. *Sport in Society, 18*(8), 968–982.
Robertson, J. W., Blain, N., & Cowan, P. (2005). The influence of friends and family vs the Simpsons: Scottish adolescents' media choices. *Learning, Media and Technology, 30*(1), 63–79.
Saunders, K. (2016). Women in the workplace: Feminism's potential impact. In M. L. Connerley & J. Wu (Eds.), *Handbook on well-being of working women* (pp. 565–575). Dordrecht: Springer Netherlands.

Singh, V., Vinnicombe, S., & James, K. (2006). Constructing a professional identity: How young female managers use role models. *Women in Management Review, 21*(1), 67–81.

Staw, B. M. (Ed.). (2004). *Psychological dimensions of organizational behavior* (3rd ed.). Englewood Cliffs, NJ: Prentice Hall.

Warhurst, R. (2011). Role modeling in manager development: Learning that which cannot be taught. *Journal of European Industrial Training, 35*(9), 874–891.

5

Complexities in the Role Model Identification Process for Educated Women from Rural India

Annu Mathew

Introduction

Role Model

A role model is defined as a cognitive construction based on the attributes of people in social roles where an individual aspires to be like those people and emulates attributes to increase the perceived similarities with those identified (Gibson, 2004). Several studies on role modelling in the past have looked at factors contributing to role model identification, the part played by role models in career advancements, the ecosystem for developing role modelling, etc. Again, most studies on role modelling are conducted in the West, thus giving us very limited knowledge

A. Mathew (✉)
Xavier School of Management, XLRI,
Jamshedpur, Jharkhand, India
e-mail: r14001@astra.xlri.ac.in

S. Vidyasagar and P. Hatti (eds.), *Leadership and Role Modelling*,
Palgrave Studies in Leadership and Followership,
https://doi.org/10.1007/978-3-319-69056-8_5

about studies conducted in the Indian context on role modelling. The traditional Indian mindset of taking on orders or imitating a leader or being a follower might create an impression that the culture in India is conducive for the formation of role models; however, there is little or no evidence to substantiate the Indian ecosystem.

While reviewing the role of ecosystem as a consideration for the process of role modelling in India, it is important to study the role of special conditions of diversity in India, such as gender, caste, religion, and the rural–urban divide and their impact on role modelling. Although there are studies on mentoring relationships in India (Pryce & Keller, 2012; Ramaswami & Dreher, 2007), and studies specific to educated urban women and mentoring (Haynes & Ghosh, 2012), there are hardly any studies pertaining to women and role modelling, especially educated women from villages in India. This chapter discusses the issues relating to Indian rural women's participation in careers owing to challenges in the role-modelling process, primarily during their upbringing as well as in their lives.

Background of the Study

Post-independence, there has been an increase in women in the workforce (Datt & Sundharam, 1999) and an increase in the employment opportunities created for women. These employment opportunities were focused on educated women residing in urban areas (Das, 2003) and not on educated women from villages. This forced the educated women from villages to migrate to urban areas for fulfilling their career aspirations. The rural background is characterised by attributes influenced by caste, culture, religion, customs, and traditions, and this has influenced the upbringing of women and is assumed to have downstream effects on their career aspirations.

Several studies in the past have established the importance of role models in supporting the socialisation process of individuals to new careers, organisations, tasks, etc. (Bell, 1970; Caldwell, Chatman, & O'Reilly, 1990; Kemper, 1968). Role models also help to create, familiarise with and define self-concept (see Bucher & Stelling, 1977; Ibarra,

1999; Super, 1963), and eventually demonstrate directions during the early stages of career and life (Gibson, 2003). Comparative studies in China can be seen in the book by Gaetano and Jacka (2004), which provides specific insights into rural women's motivations for outmigration, their work and life experiences in the city, the strategies they employ to negotiate and overcome their inferior status, how they try to shape a future, and their long-term aspirations. However, there is no mention of the relationships of these attributes with any role models.

A recent study by Peus, Braun, and Knipfer (2015) pertaining to women leaders in Asia and America described factors such as achievement orientation, learning orientation, and role models as crucial success factors for women leaders. Although there may be similarities drawn from this study, this chapter specifically explains the challenges for women from rural backgrounds to succeed in careers, be it a leadership level or an entry level due to the absence of near role models despite high achievement and learning orientation. Although studies of a similar nature have been conducted in several parts of the world, there is hardly any data on the socialisation process of educated women from rural backgrounds, where societal aspects, challenges relating to upbringing, and mobility make an impact on the role-modelling process. Furthermore, the environment that leads to identifying role models during the early stages of life and career that can affect the career goals and aspirations of rural educated women is hardly studied in the Indian context. This study thus explores the urban–rural divide, environment, societal challenges and the impact they have on the role model identification process for educated women from villages in India.

The research questions are as follows:

1. What aspects drive the role model identification process for educated women from villages in India?
2. What impact does the role model identification process have on their career aspirations?

To answer these questions, three case studies of educated women from villages from the southern part of India are chosen. These case studies examine the various life stages, career trajectories, and challenges faced as part of their role-modelling process and further impact on fulfilling their career goals. One of the primary reasons for conducting this study is that rural India constitutes 70% of the Indian population, and women in rural India are less literate compared to urban women. In 2011, 59% of rural women were literate compared to 80% of urban women who were literate (Catalyst, 2017). Owing to poor literacy levels, the number of women opting for higher education and careers is minimal. Furthermore, despite academic brilliance, improved financial status, and career aspirations, there are several obstacles such as community barriers, self-imposed restrictions, parental restrictions, societal norms, and lack of career guidance, making rural educated women a disadvantaged lot. Thus, despite being educated, the route after education is ambiguous and challenging, forcing these individuals to either choose irrelevant careers or change career tracks as they progress, having an impact on their career goals.

Structure of the Chapter

The first section is a literature review conducted to understand woman from rural India, the role-modelling ecosystem and challenges that have an impact on their educational and career goals. The second section reviews cases of women from a rural background, which were studied. The third section illustrates the situations that have an impact on the role-modelling process and its effects on meeting career goals, and this forms the contribution of this chapter to the existing body of knowledge in role modelling. The concluding section covers implications, limitations and future areas of research.

Educated Rural Indian Women and Careers

For centuries, the Indian woman has enjoyed a paradoxical status (Budhwar, 2001). While India was a country where women were worshipped as goddesses or deities, societal norms for women were different, leading to women playing a passive role. Women in rural India have limited choices for roles—such as daughter, wife, daughter-in-law, and mother—defined by the norms and structure of family and society. Although attitudes have changed considerably for the urban middle class, and an increasing number of girls have made it to careers in banking, advertising, civil services, etc. (Nath, 2000), the situation of girls from rural India has not improved. The number of women from villages who made it to the workplace in any profession in India seems to be insignificant, even though there is evidence of their contributions in agriculture and other jobs which are low paid in rural areas (Rao, 2014).

Again, although there is evidence of the transformation of urban Indian women's professional choices between the 1980s and the new millennium (Budhwar, Saini, & Bhatnagar, 2005), the situation of rural educated women, however, remained unchanged, as they had to deal with several obstacles pertaining to gender biases and gender stereotypes. The traditional view of submissive women in Indian society and patriarchal attitudes towards women still prevailed in Indian families (Bandyopadhyay, 2000), and this hindered educated rural women from fulfilling their career aspirations.

From the standpoint of the parents of a rural Indian girl child, she was to get basic education and be prepared for marriage at an early age. Even those of an affluent class considered saving money for their daughters' dowry as their main duty (Agnihotri, 2001; Sharma & Gupta, 2013). Since higher education involved money, parents were more keen on diverting savings for weddings, and there was hesitation in allowing girls to pursue higher education. This ultimately had an impact on their careers.

Role-Modelling Ecosystem

Previous research on role models emphasised that role models in the early stages of careers help individuals create, experiment, and define their self-concept (Bucher & Stelling, 1977; Ibarra, 1999; Super, 1963). As per Gibson (2003), role models are important in the early stages of life and career. There are several studies concerning role models among children and adolescents (Maccoby & Jacklin, 1974; Speizer, 1981), and among those before entering careers (Gibson & Cordova, 1999), or in early socialisation stages (Bucher & Stelling, 1977; Ibarra, 1999; Kram, 1985). Most role models identified in these studies are significant others such as supervisors, teachers, or mentors (Kram, 1985; Weiss, 1977).

As per Collins (1996), individuals select role models through the social comparison process when they want to self-improve or learn a new role or skills by choosing people who have experience in similar roles, or demonstrate such qualities, to be motivated and inspired by them (Lockwood & Kunda, 1997). Some role models are imposed by the environment (e.g. parents) and some are self-selected (Wood, 1996). As per Gibson (2003), there are 'close' or 'distant' role models based on the availability of role models in the context encountered by the individuals. The former are based on direct interactions and the latter are less visible, but have qualities sought by individuals. Availability of role models is equated with similarity of background and similarity of qualities that can be learned and emulated (Gibson, 2003). Thus, it is assumed that availability of role models with similar qualities and similar background is an important aspect for role model identification.

Role model studies are derived from two psychological theories: social learning theory (Bandura, 1977, 1986) and identification theory (Erikson, 1985; Freud, 1933; Slater, 1961). According to the social learning theory, role models are identified from the social roles played by other individuals, in order to learn new tasks, skills, attitudes, and norms, and as per the identification theory, individuals tend to identify with people who are like them, based on their perceptions about attitudes, goals, behaviours, etc. Hence, there is evidence about the process (Gibson, 2003) and stages of role modelling (Gibson, 2004), but little research examines culture and gender.

Role of Culture, Society, and Gender

According to Meyerson and Fletcher (2000), gender inequality dwells in cultural patterns and penetrates organisational systems. Culture plays a big role at the micro- and macro-levels of Indian society, and this is evident in the differences in treatment of men and women. This difference is further evident in the social role theory that posits that individuals are expected to behave as per gender roles prescribed by culture (Eagly, 1978). Indian society regards man as the 'family bread earner or breadwinner' and woman to be suited for household chores or caregiving (Budhwar & Sparrow, 2002). These cultural stereotypes about gender have an impact on the attitudes, behaviours, and goals of women from a young age, and women's careers were considered as relational based on a complex web of people and conflicting interests (Maniniero & Sullivan, 2005).

Social psychologists classify the social structures of developing and developed countries as collectivist and individualistic cultures, respectively (Greif, 1994). Collectivistic culture is characterised by the close interaction between people of specific religions or family or ethnic groups where members get involved in the lives of others, whereas outside the group there was non-cooperation. Individualistic culture is characterised by a well-integrated social structure, where the integration between groups is seamless. Since Indians are more inclined as collectivists (Sinha, 2014), the complexities created by social structures dominate the upbringing of women in the society, and the rural–urban divide further deteriorates the choices of women, thus affecting their social and personal development.

Methods

In this chapter, a multi–case study design (Stake, 1995) is applied to conduct a thorough investigation of the experiences of educated women from villages and to learn how these experiences affect the role model identification process. Case studies are rich in providing a deeper understanding of intricate and elaborate processes within the real-life context of subjects, where borders and backgrounds are not clear and there are several sources of evidence (Yin, 1984, p. 23). The approach adopted here is a descriptive case study in the narrative form (Gerring, 2004). The theoretical and empirical literature on role modelling as well as the social, cultural, and economic aspects pertaining to the upbringing of educated women in rural India are studied in this paper.

Semi-structured in-depth interviews were conducted to capture a span of 30–35 years across the subjects' childhood phase, education phase, and career phase (15 years). The challenges and experiences of subjects during these phases and the scope and process of role modelling are also covered. Data triangulation was conducted by supporting literature reviews.

Sample

Purposive sampling is chosen to study the population (Patton, 2002), and three cases are used. Purposive sampling is also known as judgement sampling and is a non-random technique that does not require underlying theories or a specific number of respondents. In purposive sampling, the researcher decides what data are required to be collected and scouts for people who can provide that information, based on their knowledge and experience (Bernard, 2002; Lewis & Sheppard, 2006). It may be considered as a sampling method to study a specific subgroup where there are similarities (http://research-methodology.net/sampling-in-primary-data-collection/purposive-sampling/). This method is also suggested as an appropriate one for fields where sources of primary data are limited. Further, this type of sampling is also considered ideal to represent a location or type pertaining to a certain criterion (Lewis & Ritchie, 2004). Since I am studying a specific group of people (rural women who encountered challenges in identifying distant role models), where sources of primary data are limited, this approach is best suited.

The rationale for a small sample size may be attributed to the findings of Charmaz (2006) and Jette, Grover, and Keck (2003). Charmaz (2006) suggested that a small study with 'modest claims' might achieve saturation faster compared to those studies that are spread across disciplines, and hence, small samples are preferred. Jette et al. (2003) suggested that expertise in an area can reduce the number of participants in any specific study.

The subjects' sociocultural background and economic conditions are homogeneous, as they are rural women from financially sound backgrounds, who received a formal education. However, the career aspirations of selected participants were different, and this difference allowed me to study the ecosystem and its impact, irrespective of careers they chose. All participants were selected based on the following criteria: (a) aged above 35 years, and having worked for more than five years; (b) had professional goals that were different from traditional choices (that is, jobs that educated women from rural areas generally undertake, typically a nine-to-five one, so that women can take care of household chores and not do anything beyond work, e.g. working in a bank or school, or for the government); (c) employed in any kind of workplace other than traditional ones; (d) faced struggles and survived challenges to make it to the workplace; and (e) married and have children and hence have adhered to societal expectations.

Data Collection

In-depth interviews were conducted with the participants and each interview lasted for more than 2 hours. Interviewing is one of the most powerful means of learning about the experiences of people and gaining meaning from them (Kvale, 1983). Two interviews were conducted in person, and one was conducted over the telephone. After the interviews were consolidated, cases were reviewed with the participants to confirm that the data I had captured properly represented their life experiences. All interviews were transcribed verbatim to ensure that the information was well-captured.

Analysis

The interview data were consolidated and coded based on keywords from interview manuscripts and grouped based on life stages to develop a descriptive case study narrative for each participant. All three cases were tabulated to identify cross-case findings and analyse the results. While there may be multiple interpretations from the text, the themes that emerged from the study are my interpretation, based on the meanings I have derived from participants' experiences (Gadamer, 1975).

Results

The participants had experience of close role models, people who were personally known to them, such as immediate family members from whom they learnt life skills or experienced certain values such as honesty, dedication, humility, patience, and commitment. These role models could not help in participants' career goal pursuits, but could help them build strong values and contributed to their upbringing. All participants shared experiences of restrictions from their religion and community, which limited their ability to reach out to others who could help them in goal attainment. The participants were however content with their achievements, since they overcame challenges over time. They were also happy that they could live up to the expectations of society, by getting married at the right age, but still have a career, although not the one they dreamt of. However, all of them felt that a close role model with professional experience could have helped them navigate the challenges they encountered in a helpful manner, thus helping them achieve their goals. Had these close role models been women, the impact would have been much higher.

It is also evident that the subjects could not identify any role models in the later stages of their career owing to challenges of communication and socialisation and their inexperience of dealing with professional role models during their early life stages. Further, the experience with family role models was at a personal level, and these were trust-based relationships, which could translate to role model identification; however, in workplaces or in professional circles, there was absence of deep relationships based on trust, leading to challenges in identifying role models for career purposes.

In the following section, individual case studies are presented, followed by cross-case findings and themes that emerged from the findings. Excerpts from the interviews are provided in Table 5.1.

Table 5.1 Excerpts from interviews

Interviewee	Background	Socialisation challenges	Gender stereotype	Unplanned events and coping mechanisms
Laila	When I was a child I wanted to become a doctor; however, because of my limited exposure and lack of access to people, I couldn't achieve my goal. There was no one to talk to about my career aspiration, as generally there was hardly any woman who had career goals or aspirations for higher studies in our village. I picked up a lot of things from my mother. She taught me the importance of religious/spiritual activities in life, how to take care of myself, good behaviour, respecting others, etc. My mother received only basic education, but she handled all her roles very well. I grew up seeing this and hence naturally she became my role model. Thus, values became more prominent in my upbringing than anything to do with career. My father was an agriculturist and was very disciplined. In some way, my father also was a role model as he had lot of confidence, I probably would have got some of those qualities from my father	I grew up in a very simple way, and there was ignorance about things happening around me. Since there were many siblings we were all together, and being a girl I couldn't express myself many a times. I was not allowed to roam around with others and was not allowed to mix with children from other backgrounds. While there was freedom to move within the friends' circle, we were kept under the observation of our mother. There was a time when I had to travel out of my state for the first time for higher education—I feared people and did not know how to interact with them, language was a barrier as well, as I did not know a neutral language to communicate	The family environment was very different; women were not asked about their careers and there was less focus on higher education. The general trend was to finish the higher secondary course and get married because that was the norm. Parents did not encourage higher education or jobs. When I got married, I didn't get any spousal support and the responsibilities that came my way after marriage restricted me from pursuing higher studies. So, I left my dreams aside and began concentrating on family and children	When I realised that I could not achieve what I dreamt about, I made up my mind to be the best in my [nursing] profession. I thought I would be the best nurse, if not a doctor. While a doctor can specialise in only one area, being a nurse I could learn about everything from head to toe, use my reasoning skills, and be an excellent nurse. This helped me to stand out in my profession. My choices were very few, so I focused on my career, and learnt a lot from my interactions with doctors and my experiences with patients. I also looked for opportunities within the hospital to learn everything new that was coming my way, be it in new ward duty or new procedures. This kind of varied exposure gave me a lot of interest in my work and what I once considered to be a bad once turned out to be an interesting one. I could not pursue higher studies in nursing, because it requires classroom trainings, and with family and kids, this was not possible, so I chose to be close to my workplace. This limited the commute time and there was complete focus on my career and family. I was not disappointed in my career, as I took on whatever came my way as challenges, struggled and put in a lot of effort to be successful. It is this positive approach to opportunities that helped me navigate through struggles. I was also very flexible and adaptable

(continued)

Table 5.1 (continued)

Interviewee	Background	Socialisation challenges	Gender stereotype	Unplanned events and coping mechanisms
Saranya	I was fascinated about becoming an advocate or a professor after observing some professionals who I thought were 'awesome'. But I was not aware of any of the professional challenges involved. My parents ensured that I got good education, even though they did not motivate me or influence in my career choices. Since I spent a lot of time with my grandmother, I got practical information about life, people, lifestyle, etc., and that helped in shaping my perspectives about life and society, but it had nothing to do with my career. When I was a child, I admired Cinderella and other characters from storybooks. Instead of real-life role models, I was living in a world of fantasy, with fairies and fictional characters. This is probably because the stories my grandmother told me during childhood influenced me	I hail from an orthodox Hindu family and was brought up in a village in the southern part of India. Ours was a big family with parents, grandmother, and my cousins. My parents were very strict and when I reached the 5th grade, I was sent to a boarding school where I was looked after by nuns, who were disciplined and strict. My religion and community put several restrictions on girls travelling outside for higher education or socialising with others	The upper-class status of my community compelled me to get married at an early age before setting up a career. The typical attitude of the community was 'your husband will decide your future and you will follow what he says'. I am married now and after my marriage, domestic responsibilities diverted me from my career dreams and I became focused on spending more time with my kids	I never felt disappointed for what I could not become and I lead a satisfied life now. I have reached somewhere (though not as professor or as advocate) and I gained many things which I never even dreamt of. Life is peaceful, comfortable, and it is satisfactory. I have a job now, I am doing well, and I can spend time with my children and see them grow. Maybe the satisfaction or contentment I am enjoying now keeps me in a situation where my imagination is enough for me to enjoy what I dreamt about, and that keeps me happy in the real world

(continued)

Table 5.1 (continued)

Interviewee	Background	Socialisation challenges	Gender stereotype	Unplanned events and coping mechanisms
Anita	I did not know what I wanted to be, and just because my father told me about several professions, I thought I should follow one of them. Now when I look back, I realise that there was very limited knowledge about careers, opportunities, or future goals. I was not convinced about fitting into professions such as engineer, doctors, teachers, banker, etc., and hence chose to be away from them from the beginning. There were no one to whom I could reach out to discuss my career options. I wanted to take my own decision about my career, but was not aware of what to decide, and I was also worried about taking risks, as there was no one to follow. Finally, I chose what my father asked me to do. I realised that I didn't have a career role model because of the very limited exposure I had had, the closed circle I was part of, and the restricted environment in which I was brought up. My grandmother was educated, and she stressed on the importance of education and played a big role in getting me interested in studies despite the restrictions that prevailed in our village and community. She became my first role model; then come my parents. My father always made me dream big and stood by my side in all things that I did, and my mother demonstrated how she could handle multiple roles	Even though there was lot of focus on education at home, the outlook was very conservative. Girls grew up mostly indoors and there was minimal socialising with outside world. There were just three places outside school where I could go: my mother's house, my cousin's place, and the church. In all these places, I was always guarded and this was the case with other girls in our village too. Since this was the norm, we did not have any complaints	The general trend in our community was to have the girls graduate and get them married off. The boys on the other hand got opportunities to study and pursue careers of their choice as they were 'future breadwinners' and girls remained at home, although many of them had career dreams. Girls were not allowed to express what they wanted to do and hence several of girls just followed what their parents told them and never ventured out to oppose any of those decisions	Everything that came my way was by chance; I made them my choices later and felt contented with what I got. I put in a lot of effort to come up in my career and this helped me compensate for the gaps in terms of support and guidance during the early stages of my life. In terms of my dreams, I was determined to get a job and I would say that I have achieved what I wanted to achieve. But if you ask me if I could have done better, I would probably say that there was potential and could have been better if there was guidance or probably someone who I could follow. In the absence of both, whatever happened was for the good, and I am content with what I have done, and where I have reached. I have no regrets as the paths I travelled were tough and making it until here is a big accomplishment

Case Studies

Case Study 1

Laila[1] is a 60-year-old nurse who recently retired after working in a large hospital for over 30 years. She was brought up with 11 siblings in a village in south India. She was a good student and dreamt of becoming a doctor. However, there were several restrictions at home which restricted her ability to reach out to people or socialise with others for career advice. There were no doctors in the family who could guide her. She did not face any pressure from her family about having a career, as the purpose of her upbringing was to get married. Hence, her career aspirations were a low-key matter in her household. She experienced several challenges, including lack of freedom of expression, and biased treatment and parental attitudes because of her gender, which restricted her from voicing her career interests. Despite these challenges, Laila got an opportunity to pursue a diploma in nursing and became a nurse. She worked in well-known hospitals and progressed in rank. She considers her mother as a role model, and learnt the values of life and self-motivation, and received religious and spiritual guidance from her. Her mother was not educated and hence could only guide her about values and religion. While these qualities have helped in several stages of her life, there was no support for professional or career development.

Laila did not have access to professional working women during the early stages of her life, and this had an impact on the choices she made about her education and career. During early life, she was confined to her own house, had limited interaction with people outside the family circle, and lacked access to information or professional success stories of women. This had an impact on role model identification and led to inexperience in identifying role models. This inexperience affected Laila even after joining the workplace. As for distant role models, there were successful people whom she knew, but she was not clear about their background or how they reached these positions, even though she considered them fortunate and admired them.

Early in her career, Laila also faced challenges with respect to communication and socialisation, since she was not very fluent in English, Hindi, or the local language where her hospital was located; this became a barrier during her interactions in social and professional circles. Thus, the initial focus in her career was to overcome language barriers and socialisation challenges. Since her upbringing had occurred in closed circles, socialisation did not come naturally and she had inhibitions in reaching out to people. Consequently, during the initial years of her career, she was focused on her job, in building credibility and trust, and becoming an expert. Again, she did not find anyone from a similar background in her workplace, which became another constraint in identifying role models.

Even though Laila faced several challenges, during our interview, she stated that she had had a successful career, having worked in extremely demanding roles and in metro cities. She always looked out for new opportunities, learnt the latest nursing procedures, and carried out her professional duties well, thus compensating through work to overcome the challenges she had faced during her upbringing. There was a doctor who guided her, and she learnt a lot from his expertise. She also looked up to him for his values and behaviour. However, the doctor was more of a mentor who could guide her than a role model. Being a nurse from a very different background, she could not identify with the doctor as their background and roles were different.

Like other women from a similar background, Laila too got married because of parental pressures soon after she got a job. After marriage, she had to focus on family and children, as there was no spousal or parental support. During this time, her focus was on family and this affected her ability to network or socialise with peers or seniors. Thus, she was not able to identify role models during the later stages of her career. Laila said that she has no disappointments in her career and is happy with the way she progressed in her career considering the challenges she faced. Laila attributed her success in the nursing profession to her positive attitude, flexibility, and adaptability.

Case Study 2

Saranya[2] is a 39-year-old law graduate currently working as an administrator in a university. She is from a conservative family and was brought up in a village in south India. Her family was financially sound and she received a good education. Saranya grew up with her grandmother, who influenced her considerably, providing perspectives on life, values, and people (such as an understanding of their background, cultures, etc.). This helped in shaping her perceptions about life and society. She was a good student and studied in a convent school, which helped her to be disciplined, since she was under the strict supervision of nuns. She dreamt of becoming a lawyer and received permission from her parents to pursue a graduate degree, but was not allowed to practise law as a profession. Her parents were focused on getting her married and were concerned about life after marriage, and did not pay much attention to her career aspirations. Her religion and community also imposed restrictions in terms of travel and interactions with others, thus affecting her career goals. Since there was no pressure or motivation to do anything big, naturally, she did not feel the need for a role model.

Saranya was always influenced by fictional characters from storybooks (e.g. Cinderella) and had a fascination for them. These characters influenced her behaviour and sometimes her thoughts. She attributes this to the influence of stories told by her grandmother during her childhood.

From a career perspective, Saranya was fascinated by the work of lawyers and professors but had little knowledge about these professions, though she had heard about a few male professionals. This was mere superficial knowledge and she had no clarity on how to pursue a career or understand the challenges of working, since she did interact closely with any professionals from this field. Even though she got a degree in law, she could not pursue a career in law, due to familial and societal challenges. She does not, however, have any regrets that she chose a career that was less demanding, so that she could focus on her children and family. She had to sacrifice her career dreams so that she could spend more time with her children, since she did not get any spousal support to manage responsibilities at home and at work. Saranya said that she admires the qualities of certain people and emulates them in her life, where she performs several roles, but she has no knowledge of their background and no close interactions with them; thus, it was emotionally difficult for her to identify or accept them as role models.

Case Study 3

Anita[3] is a 39-year-old human resources professional, who was born and brought up in a village in the southern part of India. She was a good student and got the foundation for education from her father and grandmother, who were educated, and her mother influenced her in terms of values and behaviours. Her family was financially sound, and there were no restrictions in terms of education. She went to a local school, but moved to the city for higher studies. Anita had support from her grandmother and father to pursue her education, even though there were challenges with respect to socialising with others and restrictions imposed by the community, owing to her gender. She considers her parents and grandmother as role models because they gave her the freedom to dream big and venture out to do things within the boundaries imposed by the community, religion, and society. During her childhood, she admired two women who worked as civil service officers and was fascinated by the way they had succeeded in their careers. Anita dreamt of joining the civil services, but had no clarity with respect to choosing courses or opportunities she could pursue to achieve this. She wanted to be different from other girls in her community who had gotten married at an early age because of family pressure.

Anita lacked guidance in achieving her career dreams and she could not reach out to others. Her interactions with cousins who stayed in cities were minimal; thus, she was not able to have conversations about career. It was not common in rural households for girls to talk about careers, because the general notion was to get them settled in marriage; hence, girls rarely initiated such conversations. Anita could not socialise with students in the colleges (located in cities) where she studied, as they were from an urban background and had had a different upbringing. Accessing alumni from school and college was also difficult because of the lack of women in corporate careers.

Anita chose the path that came her way and got a job in human resources, even though she got degree in finance. She said that although she had done well in her career, she felt that things would have been better had there been a close role model. Even in the workplace, Anita did not find a role model due to her inexperience in role model identification—she had inhibitions in reaching out to people and several barriers to overcome, such as coping with new locations, new workplaces, and meeting the demands of the job, which made her focus on her career and establish herself. It was a struggle initially and she learnt from her experiences, characterising her career establishment as a self-made process. Although she appreciates certain qualities of her colleagues and friends, she confirmed that she was not able to pinpoint anyone as a role model.

Cross-Case Findings: Challenges in Role Model Identification at Different Life Stages

First, challenges in the role-modelling process at the various life stages of women are explored in the context of the cases presented, and emergent themes are discussed. Each theme represents cross-sample findings based on data obtained from interviewees. Second, the linkage of the themes with other studies in the extant literature is highlighted.

Challenges in Role Model Identification in Early Life and Its Impact on Career Goals

All the three women interviewed described their career dreams as being inspired by people, events, or motivational stories they had come across in their lives. They also explained the various challenges they had to face to turn their dreams into reality. The interviewees lacked information and direction with respect to choice of careers, choice of subjects to study, and making career decisions. It is evident that they lacked adequate guidance to fulfil their career dreams, and this could be attributed to the lack of mentors or lack of near role models within the circle of people they knew. The villages where they grew up did not have many people who had made it big in their careers, and there were not many women who had followed this path. There were role models in their life during childhood, and this was likely a family member—mother, father, or grandparents—or distant role models such as fictional characters, and these individuals helped shape the subjects' values and behaviours, but with minimal or no influence in shaping careers or guidance about a professional life.

Social Challenges Affecting Role Identification During Growing-Up Phase

Role modelling is a cognitive process where individuals actively observe, adapt, and reject the attributes of various role models (Bucher & Stelling, 1977; Ibarra, 1999), and socialisation plays an important role in the process. Bugental and Grusec (1998, p. 366) observe that socialisation includes the ability and motivation to acquire individual and culturally shared competencies at social, emotional, and cognitive levels. Society, religion, and family members influenced the subjects' upbringing and imposed several restrictions in the socialisation process, thus affecting their ability or freedom to meet people outside the closed circle. The subjects were brought up in restricted environments, forcing them to stick to a closed group of friends, siblings, or cousins who had minimal education or lacked exposure to the workplace per se. Social experience and background are prerequisites for the role-modelling process (Kulik & Ambrose, 1992) and any developmental relationship that has an impact on career requires social experience and similarity of background. Thus, any restriction in the social environment limits possibilities in the role model search. Even though the women were brought up in large families, there were limitations on travel opportunities and choices for higher education. They were compelled by their parents and the community to get married immediately after finishing their education, which affected their careers, and hence, they were not able to identify opportunities for socialisation for personal or professional development.

Gender Stereotypes and Downstream Challenges During Adulthood in Role Model Identification

The subjects faced several challenges grounded in the culture and beliefs of the primarily male-dominated society. These attitudes are so deep-rooted that despite the changes in the environment (subjects worked in urban areas), they were unable to identify role models for professional development because of their inexperience in socialisation or challenges pertaining to the new environments they were exposed to. While it is acknowledged that urban women also face these types of challenges, the closed societies in villages are more stringent about following rituals and customs. The women interviewed felt that they had very limited opportunities compared to men or their male siblings, as men were considered future breadwinners and could pursue any opportunity they wanted, but women were supposed to get married and take on more docile roles. Kulkarni (2002) highlights that social stereotypes, gendered role expectations, individual prejudices, and social forces promote women's image as secondary to that of men and discourage women from aspiring for careers.

Undertaking family responsibilities after marriage is another aspect that had an impact on the role-modelling process. After their children were born, the subjects' families took priority over their jobs; hence, they did not have opportunities to network in professional circles to identify role models. This was either because of their personal choice in focusing on their families, or because of lack of support from spouses or parents in bringing up children. The duty of married women in rural India was to obey husbands and please their in-laws (Gangoli & Rew, 2011); hence, the challenges of being a woman forced the subjects—educated women from rural India—to accept things that came their way and not venture out to seek role models to support them in their careers.

Compensating for Challenges Faced During Pursuit of Goals

According to Alfred Adler (1964), a weakness in one area is compensated by succeeding in another. The interviewees overcompensated by giving their best to the paths that came their way—the courses they studied or the jobs they were in—thus making good the loss from challenges faced in achieving their dream careers because of the lack of adequate support or societal restrictions. The determination to excel, along with the aim to make an impact, helped in bringing success in the areas in which they studied or worked. While some compensated in the professional and educational space, others focused on family and children.

Discussion

The purpose of this study is to explore in depth the challenges educated women from rural India face in identifying role models.

The first theme to emerge from the data is the career goals of subjects during childhood, the challenges they faced due to lack of information and the absence of a close role model with whom they could identify to achieve their goals. Family members who were role models provided adequate support—it is notable to learn how they picked up values and behaviours, and knowledge about culture and society from their family members—even though the subjects lacked close professional role models to help in their career aspirations. Most parents were involved in agriculture or small-scale businesses with limited exposure to workplaces and even working parents, of whom there was a small segment; there was little help one could get, as social and cultural aspects dominated the upbringing of women. The absence of close professional role models forced the interviewees to change their career plans and accept unintended ones. Furthermore, the results highlight how difficult it was for women to voice their career aspirations; however, once they obtained jobs, they put in significant effort to achieve their career objectives. To elaborate, in an ecosystem where the career aspirations of women were not given importance but they were allowed to study, their aspirations became stronger, and although they could not pursue the jobs they wanted, the women made additional efforts to come out of such an ecosystem by accepting the career paths that came their way and navigating through their career.

The second theme that emerges is the impact of the socialisation process during childhood on role model identification. The absence of social experiences during childhood or an encouraging background that allowed for freedom to interact with others was a barrier that hindered women from reaching out to others or experiencing role models from a professional background across their life stages. Furthermore, it is interesting that these women point to the restrictions imposed by their religion and society in shaping their career dreams. To give an example, Saranya was not allowed to take up courses in premier schools outside her home state due to travel restrictions imposed by religion and society. These restrictions resulted in limitations on learning new languages or building trusted relationships with others, thus creating obstacles in identifying role models the women could trust and in building professional connections.

The third theme that emerges from the data is how gender stereotypes constrained role model identification. New information emerged about how communities had defined certain paths for women, and they had to follow them instinctively, thus limiting their opportunities, compared to men with a similar background. Communities defining the women's course of action can be seen in instances of getting married at an early age, restricting travel for education or, in some cases, careers, and expecting women to manage both career and family responsibilities. The stereotypical expectations for women to manage family and children required them to prioritise family over careers right from childhood, thus restraining them from networking or engaging in activities that would help in career development. The exclusion of women from such informal networks became barriers to career progression (Gupta, Koshal, & Koshal, 1998), posing challenges to the role model identification process at a cognitive level. The primary focus of getting married at an early age became another challenge for these women; while men had a say in these decisions, women were not free to express their opinions regarding these life decisions. Further, the situation did not change for the subjects even after marriage, as parenting was the biggest responsibility and they received less support, either parental or spousal, thus affecting the role model identification process.

According to Gelatt (1989), unplanned events are not only inevitable but also desirable. Risk-taking, optimism, flexibility, persistence, and curiosity are skills discussed by Mitchell, Levin, and Krumboltz (1999) to generate, recognise, and incorporate chance events or unplanned events in career development. It is evident that these subjects demonstrated these skills and progressed in their careers or education; they managed to achieve success in the later part of their lives and hence were not disappointed about opportunities lost. One example is Laila studying for a diploma in nursing—it was an opportunity that came her way through a reference and she had to travel to a different (and distant) state in the country—which demonstrates her risk-taking ability and optimism. Saranya accepting a job in a different country without any prior experience of living or working in an urban working environment with people from different countries is another example of optimism, flexibility, and risk-taking attitude.

Identification with a distant role model came up in two cases, but the subjects did not mention that these role models had an influence or impact on their careers. This points to the fact that while the women identified distant role models, they did not intellectually accept them as role models because of the absence of a significant impact. At an emotional level, these role models helped them in having a goal or dream about careers, but there is no evidence of the influence they have on the subjects' professional growth, and this could be a possible area for future research.

Similarity of background is another theme that emerges from the study. Identification of close role models is attributed to similarity of background of subjects and role models, which helps develop trust-based relationships and role model identification.

The synergy between role modelling and the individual's potential would have an impact on outcomes such as making right career choices, choosing the right educational programme to achieve career dreams or navigating career challenges. This explains the need for close professional role models for educated women from rural backgrounds, and hence, this study provides us with an opportunity to contemplate about possible outcomes for women had they had chosen close role models, which could be a potential area for study in future.

Implications for Research and Practice

The findings of this study have definite implications for role modelling among women and challenges pertaining to the same, and interventions and research related to role modelling. The studies on educated urban women and mentoring (Haynes & Ghosh, 2012) and career opportunities for educated women residing in urban areas (Das, 2003) have actively discussed professional development and career support for urban women and their impact on career outcomes. The intervention of a policy by an Indian state to enhance the aspirations of girls through the role model effect in villages has been studied (Beaman, Duflo, Pande, & Topalova, 2012), but experiences that had an impact on the role-modelling process for rural educated girls with strong career goals are not found in any previous studies. The findings from this study can be used to (a) expand the understanding of the role-modelling process for women, (b) postulate the challenges faced by women from a rural background in their careers and attribute any of their career gaps to challenges they faced during childhood, (c) elaborate on the experiences of women from villages in their quest to accomplish their aspirations by challenging the status quo and sociocultural restrictions, and (d) evaluate the relationship between social, cultural, and economic conditions involved in role modelling or any other research in social science that studies the impact of social, cultural, and economic conditions on career development with similar demographics.

For practitioners, this study can help understand the background of women employees who have lacked career support in workplaces and provide additional interventions, serve as a source for coaching women in workplace make them aware of the resilience of women employees and how they can contribute to workplaces given additional support, and, above all, enable managers to adopt a creative approach to handle women employees from similar backgrounds by offering additional opportunities for learning and development.

Limitations of the Study

The findings of this study must be reviewed in the context of certain limitations in the development of cases. First, the data are based on interviews with the women who have reported their experiences and challenges. There could be richer data available, had interviews been conducted with parents or siblings to elaborate on the understanding of experiences pertaining to sociocultural backgrounds. The choice of participants is another limitation—they were chosen because of their specific employment status, age, and choice of workplace, but they had different careers, education, and capabilities. The sample did not include women who had chosen traditional careers. Homogeneity of the economic background of participants is another limitation; diversity of economic background would have provided additional insights on the impact of economic or financial background on role modelling. The sample size is small because of the inductive and case study–based method, and the choice of purposive sampling may have an inherent bias, which could also be a limitation.

Notes

1. Name changed to protect privacy.
2. Name changed to protect privacy.
3. Name changed to protect privacy.

References

Adler, A. (1964). *Individual psychology of Alfred Adler* (Vol. 1154). New York, NY: Harper Collins.

Agnihotri, S. (2001). Declining infant and child mortality in India: How do girl children fare? *Economic and Political Weekly, 36*(3), 228–233.

Bandura, A. (1977). Self-efficacy: Toward a unifying theory of behavioral change. *Psychological Review, 84*(2), 191–215.

Bandura, A. (1986). *Social foundations of thought and action: A social cognitive theory*. Englewood Cliffs, NJ: Prentice-Hall.

Bandyopadhyay, D. (2000). Gender and governance in India. *Economic and Political Weekly, 32*(31), 2696–2699.

Beaman, L., Duflo, E., Pande, R., & Topalova, P. (2012). Female leadership raises aspirations and educational attainment for girls: A policy experiment in India. *Science, 335*(6068), 582–586.

Bell, A. P. (1970). Role modelship and interaction in adolescence and young adulthood. *Developmental Psychology, 2*(1), 123–128.

Bernard, H. R. (2002). *Research methods in anthropology: Qualitative and quantitative methods*, (3rd ed.). Walnut Creek, CA: Altamira Press.

Bucher, R., & Stelling, J. G. (1977). *Becoming professional*. Beverly Hills, CA: SAGE.

Budhwar, P. (2001). Doing business in India. *Thunderbird International Business Review, 43*(4), 549–568.

Budhwar, P. S., & Sparrow, P. R. (2002). Strategic HRM through the cultural looking glass: Mapping the cognition of British and Indian managers. *Organization Studies, 23*(4), 599–638.

Budhwar, P. S., Saini, D. S., & Bhatnagar, J. (2005). Women in management in the new economic environment: The case of India. *Asia Pacific Business Review, 11*(2), 179–193.

Bugental, D. B., & Grusec, J. E. (1998). Socialization processes. In N. Eisenberg (Ed.), *Handbook of child psychology (Vol. 3): Social, emotional and personality development*, (6th ed., pp. 366–428). Hoboken, NJ: Wiley.

Caldwell, D. F., Chatman, J. A., & O'Reilly, C. A. (1990). Building organizational commitment: A multifirm study. *Journal of Occupational Psychology, 63*(3), 245–261.

Catalyst. (2017, June 27). Quick take: Women in the labour force in India. *Catalyst*. Retrieved on September 24, 2017 from http://www.catalyst.org/knowledge/women-workforce-india.

Charmaz, K. (2006). The power of names. *Journal of Contemporary Ethnography, 35*(4), 396–399.

Collins, R. L. (1996). For better or worse: The impact of upward social comparison on self-evaluations. *Psychological Bulletin, 119*(1), 51–69.

Das, K. B. (2003). Employment scenario under globalisation. In R. Datt (Ed.), *Second generation economic reforms in India* (pp. 151–163). New Delhi, India: Deep & Deep.

Datt, R., & Sundharam, K. P. H. (1999). *Indian Economy*. New Delhi, India: S. Chand.

Eagly, A. H. (1978). Sex differences in influenceability. *Psychological Bulletin, 85*(1), 86–116.

Erikson, E. H. (1985). *Childhood and society* (35th Anniversary ed.). New York, NY: W.W. Norton.

Freud, S. (1933). *New introductory lectures on psychoanalysis* (J. Strachey, Trans.). New York, NY: Norton.

Gadamer, H. G. (1975). *Truth and method* (G. Barden & J. Cumming, Trans.). New York, NY: Seabury.

Gaetano, A. M., & Jacka, T. (2004). *On the move: Women and rural-to-urban migration in contemporary China*. New York, NY: Columbia University Press.

Gangoli, G., & Rew, M. (2011). Mothers-in-law against daughters-in-law: Domestic violence and legal discourses around mother-in-law violence against daughters-in-law in India. *Women's Studies International Forum, 34*(5), 420–429.

Gelatt, H. B. (1989). Positive uncertainty: A new decision-making framework for counseling. *Journal of Counseling Psychology, 36*(2), 252–256.

Gerring, J. (2004). What is a case study and what is it good for? *American Political Science Review, 98*(02), 341–354.

Gibson, D. E. (2003). Developing the professional self-concept: Role model construals in early, middle, and late career stages. *Organization Science, 14*(5), 591–610.

Gibson, D. E. (2004). Role models in career development: New directions for theory and research. *Journal of Vocational Behavior, 65*(1), 134–156.

Gibson, D. E., & Cordova, D. I. (1999). Women's and men's role models: The importance of exemplars. In A. J. Murrell, F. J. Crosby, & R. J. Ely (Eds.), *Mentoring dilemmas: Developmental relationships within multicultural organizations* (pp. 121–141). Mahwah, NJ: Erlbaum.

Greif, A. (1994). Cultural beliefs and the organization of society: A historical and theoretical reflection on collectivist and individualist societies. *Journal of Political Economy, 102*(5), 912–950.

Gupta, A., Koshal, M., & Koshal, R. K. (1998). Women managers in India: Challenges and opportunities. *Equal Opportunities International, 17*(8), 14–26.

Haynes, R. K., & Ghosh, R. (2012). Towards mentoring the Indian organizational woman: Propositions, considerations, and first steps. *Journal of World Business, 47*(2), 186–193.

Ibarra, H. (1999). Provisional selves: Experimenting with image and identity in professional adaptation. *Administrative Science Quarterly, 44*(4), 764–791.

Jette, D. U., Grover, L., & Keck, C. P. (2003). A qualitative study of clinical decision making in recommending discharge placement from the acute care setting. *Physical Therapy, 83*(3), 224–236.

Kemper, T. D. (1968). Reference groups, socialization and achievement. *American Sociological Review, 33*(1), 31–45.

Kram, K. E. (1985). *Mentoring at work: Developmental relationships in organizational life*. Glenview, IL: Scott Foresman.

Kulik, C. T., & Ambrose, M. L. (1992). Personal and situational determinants of referent choice. *Academy of Management Review, 17*(2), 212–237.

Kulkarni, S. S. (2002). Women and professional competency: A survey report. *Indian Journal of Training and Development, 32*(2), 11–16.

Kvale, S. (1983). The qualitative research interview: A phenomenological and a hermeneutical mode of understanding. *Journal of Phenomenological Psychology, 14*(2), 171–196.

Lewis, J., & Ritchie, J. (2004). Generalizing from qualitative research. In J. Ritchie & J. Lewis (Eds.), *Qualitative research practice: A guide for social science students and researchers* (pp. 263–286). London, UK: SAGE.

Lewis, J. L., & Sheppard, S. R. (2006). Culture and communication: Can landscape visualization improve forest management consultation with indigenous communities? *Landscape and Urban Planning, 77*(3), 291–313.

Lockwood, P., & Kunda, Z. (1997). Superstars and me: Predicting the impact of role models on the self. *Journal of Personality and Social Psychology, 73*(1), 91–103.

Maccoby, E. E., & Jacklin, C. N. (1974). *The psychology of sex differences* (Vol. 1). Stanford, CA: Stanford University Press.

Mainiero, L. A., & Sullivan, S. E. (2005). Kaleidoscope careers: An alternate explanation for the 'opt-out' revolution. *The Academy of Management Executive, 19*(1), 106–123.

Meyerson, D. E., & Fletcher, J. K. (2000). A modest manifesto for shattering the glass ceiling. *Harvard Business Review, 78*(1), 126–136.

Mitchell, K. E., Levin, S., & Krumboltz, J. D. (1999). Planned happenstance: Constructing unexpected career opportunities. *Journal of Counselling & Development, 77*(2), 115–124.

Nath, D. (2000). Gently shattering the glass ceiling: Experiences of Indian women managers. *Women in Management Review, 15*(1), 44–52.

Patton, M. (2002). *Qualitative evaluation and research methods* (3rd ed.). Newbury Park, CA: SAGE.

Peus, C., Braun, S., & Knipfer, K. (2015). On becoming a leader in Asia and America: Empirical evidence from women managers. *Leadership Quarterly, 26*(1), 55–67.

Pryce, J., & Keller, T. E. (2012). An investigation of volunteer-student relationship trajectories within school-based youth mentoring programs. *Journal of Community Psychology, 40*(2), 228–248.

Ramaswami, A., & Dreher, G. F. (2007). The benefits associated with workplace mentoring relationships. In T. D. Allen & L. T. Eby (Eds.), *The Blackwell handbook of mentoring: A multiple perspectives approach* (pp. 212–231). Malden, MA: Blackwell.

Rao, N. (2014). Caste, kinship, and life course: Rethinking women's work and agency in rural South India. *Feminist Economics, 20*(3), 78–102.

Sharma, B. R., & Gupta, M. (2013). Gender based violence in India: A never-ending phenomenon. *Journal of International Women's Studies, 6*(1), 114–123.

Sinha, J. B. (2014). *Psycho-social analysis of the Indian mindset*. New Delhi, India: Springer.

Slater, P. E. (1961). Parental role differentiation. *American Journal of Sociology, 67*(3), 296–311.

Speizer, J. J. (1981). Role models, mentors, and sponsors: The elusive concepts. *Signs, 6*(4), 692–712.

Stake, R. E. (1995). *The art of case study research*. Thousand Oaks, CA: SAGE.

Super, D. E. (1963). Toward making self-concept theory operational. In D. E. Super, R. Starishevsky, N. Matlin, & J. P. Jordaan (Eds.), *Career development: Self concept theory* (pp. 7–32). New York, NY: College Entrance Examination Board.

Weiss, H. M. (1977). Subordinate imitation of supervisory behavior: The role of modeling in organizational socialization. *Organizational Behavior and Human Performance, 19*(1), 89–105.

Wood, J. V. (1996). What is social comparison and how should we study it? *Personality and Social Psychology Bulletin, 22*(5), 520–537.

Yin, R. (1984). *Case study research: Design and methods* (1st ed.). Beverly Hills, CA: SAGE.

Section III

Practitioners' Perspectives

6

Role Modelling as a Means of Transformative Growth

Kshitij Sharma

Some time ago, a coaching client of mine, who is the CEO of a mid-sized automobile servicing company, told me that he was experiencing a great deal of attrition in his organisation. He complained about the attitude of a few supervisors, who had stalled operations because they were unhappy with management. On probing further, I found out that the supervisors were not happy with CEO's communication style since he had the habit of scolding them in front of their subordinates. The CEO agreed that he needed to change his communication style, but admitted that he found it very difficult to keep his cool when he saw a mistake or was faced with insubordination. I asked him if he knew of anyone who could (and did) handle such situations better. He promptly responded that his wife, his business partner (and director of the company),

K. Sharma (✉)
Coach Kshitij, Bengaluru, India
e-mail: kshitij@coachkshitij.com

S. Vidyasagar and P. Hatti (eds.), *Leadership and Role Modelling*,
Palgrave Studies in Leadership and Followership,
https://doi.org/10.1007/978-3-319-69056-8_6

handled such situations with ease and grace. I asked him if he wanted to role model his wife's behaviour. He agreed, and, in a few months, the situation had turned around. He changed his behaviour towards by changing his communication style during conflict situations.

Another coaching client, a young and dynamic executive, who had graduated from a premier Indian business school, was appointed to a management position in a multinational investment banking firm. He told me that he was not able to cope with the enormous amount of work. He spent almost 16 hours a day at work and worked during the weekends. During our discussion, this client decided to role model his batch mate, who too had joined the same company in a similar role. The batch mate was performing well while spending around 10 hours a day at work, in addition to maintaining an excellent work–life balance. A sustained effort of three months by the client brought about a substantial difference in his work–life balance.

The two cases above are mere examples. There are several people in similar situations, who see others accomplishing with ease the things they struggle with. It could be any behaviour, be it handling challenging conversations or delegating work effectively or maintaining a good work–life balance or public speaking.

A Quicker Solution

It is possible for behaviour to be modelled and learnt quickly through role modelling, which is an apt method for those who are very clear about the outcomes they desire and seek to grow in their lives. It is a very powerful tool used by people who would like to acquire certain skills, habits, and qualities that they admire in their role models. This is the simplest approach to succeed in an area in which you wish to excel.

Role modelling is about identifying a role model, a person/s you admire and want to emulate, and then very keenly observing or discovering their behaviour, thoughts, actions, body language, etc., and learning from them. This is one of the quickest ways to learn something and obtain results. You will find out more about how to practise role modelling later in this chapter.

When you are role modelling, you are continuously and constructively focused on the desired result. The emphasis is therefore not on what is *not* required; it is instead on what *is* required.

The Starting Point

The first step is to become aware of your focus. The focus decides the direction in which you are heading and the direction decides your success. It is imperative that you head in the right direction to succeed, for which it is very important that you are focused on the desired direction and not against it.

Imagine, deep within, you actually want to be a very powerful public speaker but your constant focus is on your inability to speak effectively. What will you experience? Confidence or fear? Obviously, you will experience what you are focusing on which, in the above example, is fear.

Once, someone asked Mother Teresa to join them in their protest against the war in Vietnam, to which she politely refused. She said that she would not join in any activity that was against war; instead, she would be very happy to join any efforts for peace in Vietnam. Mother Teresa made a clear statement that one's area of focus decides the outcome.

Many people come to me with a desire to get rid of their fear of public speaking or to overcome some bad habit, and my question to them is, 'What is your desired state?' If you have a clear picture of the desired state in your mind then your success is almost guaranteed. Ralph Waldo Emerson said, 'The ancestor to every action is a thought' (BrainyQuote, 2016). So, it is important that one's thoughts are in the right direction.

One chooses a role model based on qualities that one admires and wants to possess in oneself. The journey is about identifying certain qualities and attributes that one values, then identifying someone who best possesses such qualities and attributes, and making that person one's role model. This can be done through two ways, by observation and by asking (if the role model is real and alive).

A role model can be anyone—dead or alive, male or female, real or fictitious—it does not matter. What matters is their attributes, qualities, and behaviour, which one wants to emulate. Many people ask me what happens when the role model is not within reach, how can one still emulate their qualities and attributes? This is a very pertinent question. As you will read later in this chapter, what matters are the thought processes, beliefs, and values of the role model, for those are what drive the desired and much-admired actions or behaviour.

To role model someone, it is not necessary to talk to them. One can learn about them (their actions, emotions, thoughts, values, and beliefs) through books, internet research, or talking to people who have worked with them. It is also not necessary that you emulate your role model in entirety. Rather, it is recommended that one chooses specific behaviour that you want to emulate and model only that. For example, I love the assertiveness of Gandhi, the energy and body language of Tony Robbins, the serenity of Dr. Wayne Dyer, the composure of Dr. Deepak Chopra, the focus of Sachin Tendulkar, and the wisdom of Sri Bhagavan, founder of Oneness University. That makes all the above listed people my role models in some way or the other.

Ideally, one should have only one role model for modelling a particular attribute at any given point of time. If you consider multiple role models for a particular attribute, it is advisable to finally focus on only one role model at any given point, for this ensures more focus and less confusion. One of my coaching clients was unable to be consistent about her exercise regime. She could not persist with her morning exercise ritual for more than a week. As a part of our coaching, she considered two of her friends as possible role models. Both had very consistent and strict exercise regimes. When she interviewed them individually, she discovered that one of them was consistent because he had made a commitment to himself, after an early death of a family member due to ill health. The second friend was consistent because she wanted to look good. On probing further, my client discovered that her self-confidence always increased when she looked good. So, she could relate more to the second friend and hence made her a role model for this behaviour.

If, for some reason, you are not able to find a role model, or if the role model is not available for communication, you should continue to search for a role model, for, with right focus and continuous effort, the right role model may just manifest.

Prerequisites to Role Modelling

Like any tall building has a strong foundation, to successfully model someone, one needs to possess some basic attributes.

Attitude Towards Learning

The story of Nan-in, a Japanese master during the Meiji era (1868–1912), is told in *Zen Flesh, Zen Bones*, compiled by Paul Reps and Nyogen Senzaki (1957). Nan-in received a university professor who came to inquire about Zen. Nan-in served tea. He poured till his visitor's cup was full and then continued pouring. The professor watched the overflow until he could no longer restrain himself. 'It is overfull. No more will go in!' he said. 'Like this cup,' Nan-in replied, 'you are full of your own opinions and speculations. How can I show you Zen unless you first empty your cup?'

Our growth in life is directly proportional to our willingness to learn constantly and our willingness to learn depends upon our attitude towards learning. This is the first and most fundamental principle to succeed of life. If we are so full with all that we already know, then our capacity to take in new learnings diminishes considerably. Every day, when we wake up, we have a choice to consider ourselves as a know-all or as a beginner who is still learning every single day. The choice is ours. If we choose to view ourselves as a learner, our world view changes and we seek opportunities in every moment to learn and grow in our lives.

When you are modelling someone, this attitude is a must, for only then will you have the keenness to observe every behaviour of your role model. Observation plays a big role in successful role modelling Therefore, if you do not have the inclination to learn, you will not be able to observe effectively.

One of my clients, who is in a senior leadership position in an IT firm, observed that several of his team members, especially from the younger generation, stayed away from him. After introspecting, he realised that they were afraid of him because he never smiled and always had a very serious demeanour. He wanted to change this perception, because, in reality, he wanted to be friends with his colleagues, and did not want them to think that he was a serious, unfriendly person. He modelled one of his own friends, of a similar age and seniority, and very popular with his team. The first thing he needed to do was to shed his inhibitions and be open to learning from his friend. The attitude to learn determines one's speed in the journey of growth.

Clarity About Goals

This 'lifelong learner' approach comes when one has the big picture in mind. So, what is the big picture? A very significant aspect in our life's journey is the knowledge of what we want to achieve. Sometimes, people are ready to travel that extra mile when the outcome they are looking for is crystal clear in their minds. This outcome serves as a motivation.

Here is a real-life story of the great swimmer Florence Chadwick, which Randy Alcorn (2010) has told eloquently. In 1952, she took on herself the arduous task of crossing the Pacific Ocean from Catalina Island till the shore of mainland California—around 26 miles. She had, earlier, become the first lady to swim across the English Channel. The weather was foggy and it was very cold. She could hardly see anything around her including the boats accompanying her. Despite that, she swam for about 15 hours. Unfortunately, she started feeling exhausted after 15 hours of constant swimming in the chilly weather. She requested to be taken out of the water before she had completed swimming the distance. Her mother, who was accompanying her in a boat alongside, told her she was close and that she could make it. Florence however just stopped swimming and had to be pulled out of the water.

Only when she sat on the boat did she realise that the shore was just half a mile away. Later, she told the press at a news conference, 'All I could see was the fog. I think, if I could have seen the coast, I would have made it.'

Two months later, Florence got back into the water for a second attempt. She swam for 26 miles in a straight line. The same thick fog reappeared, but Florence did not allow it to stop her as she focused on a mental image of the destination. Florence Chadwick thus became the first woman to swim across Catalina Channel, beating the men's record by two hours!

She never lost sight of the destination because she had an image of the coast in her mind, and that brought her success. Consider Florence Chadwick's words: 'I think if I could have seen the coast, I would have made it.' Lack of clarity is the fog in our lives, and the image of coast line is the clearly defined goal.

Stephen R. Covey, the famous author of *The Seven Habits of Highly Effective People*, claims that you should always begin with the end in mind. This means that you are completely aware of the direction in which you are heading. If you are clear about your goals in life, you will be like an arrow; else, you will be like a feather. The feather is at the mercy of the direction of the wind, whereas an arrow is always aware of its target.

For someone to effectively use role modelling as a tool for self-development, it is imperative that they are very clear about their priorities and goals in life. Only then can one pick the desired role model and make substantial progress.

There is a common myth that employees need to work on the goals identified by their organisation and that's all. Very seldom have I come across employees who set their own goals, which are above and beyond those set by their organisations. They don't set personal goals, as they do not have the holistic bigger picture of their career aspirations in the long run.

Self-Awareness

There is a saying that you start from where you are and not where you would like to be. The journey of self-development begins from self-awareness.

As I mentioned earlier in this chapter, role modelling is all about first identifying a role model and then keenly observing their behaviour, thoughts, actions, body language, and so on. But before you do that, it is essential that you are highly self-aware. You will be able to observe your role model's behaviour and emulate only if you are a keen observer of your own self.

Usually, I give the following set of questions to the persons I coach, to enhance their self-awareness and to offer them a perspective of where they stand today vis-à-vis where they want to be.

- What are my life goals?
- What are my top strengths?
- What are the specific qualities that I want to develop so I can achieve my life goals?
- In what degree do I possess these qualities today?
- What are the skills that I want to hone so that I can achieve my life goals?
- What is my current proficiency of the skills I want to develop?

Finding the Right Role Model

The journey of role modelling starts by identifying your goals. Once you have identified your goals and your self-awareness is high, you will soon realise that there are certain things that you have already achieved and there are certain things that you wish you had.

One of my coaching clients was the country head of a large pharma company. He was a highly qualified, hardworking, and successful person. He used to work late in the night during weekdays and work on weekends too. His problem, as perceived by him, was lack of quality time with himself and his family because he was overworked. The impact was high stress, health problems, and dissatisfied family members. His problem could well be considered as one of poor time management. I asked him to identify one person whom he knew well and whom he could consider as his role model in this context. He immediately identified his friend who was a CEO of another company and who, in his opinion, managed things very well as he appeared to have all the time needed to do things which he loved, right from playing golf to travelling with family.

Identifying the right person as a role model for certain desired qualities is, therefore, a very significant step.

Role Modelling in Practice

My coaching client, who identified his friend to be his role model for time management, then asked me how he should go about role modelling. That is a very pertinent question. And it is a question which many people ask me.

'Observing' and 'questioning' are the two most significant ways of effective role modelling. If the person is alive and accessible, one can ask relevant and pertinent questions to understand what empowers them to do the thing that you wish to model.

In this context, the age-old iceberg model is significant. What is visible to everyone from outside is someone's success. The results are what people see, as well as someone's behaviour or actions. The question to ask is what lies beneath those actions or behaviour? Like in an iceberg, the visible part is less than 10% of the entire structure. The most significant part is below the surface; it is not visible from outside but it drives the entire structure. So, 'what is the secret of someone's success?' is an important question for a person who is role modelling someone else. The various factors that lead to someone's success include their behaviour, emotions, thinking patterns, values, and most significantly, their beliefs.

Behaviour

The results we achieve in our life are dependent on the actions we take. Our action or behaviour is visible to all. For example, consider someone who is very good at building and maintaining relationships. Now, this is a result that people can see from outside. If you observe closely, you will find that this person is taking certain actions to build good relationships; these actions could include addressing people by their names, greeting them proactively, understanding their needs, appreciating them, acknowledging them, maintaining a calm and composed behaviour during conflicts, and so on. This behaviour can be identified through observation.

Now, the next question would be, 'Why do we do what we do?'

Emotions

To a great extent, one's actions depend on one's emotions. If you are feeling good, you will behave one way, whereas, if you are feeling bad, you will behave differently. Actions emerging from fear will be very different from actions emerging from self-confidence.

Thus, in the above example of the person who is good at relationship building, if you delve deeply and ask him about his emotions when he meets people, you may discover that he is someone who loves to meet people, and who always get excited by the idea of working in teams. The emotion leading to the behaviour of making an extra effort to build relationships could be love or excitement or gratitude or empathy or anything else.

Now, the next question to ask here is, 'What creates these emotions in our life?'

Thinking

Our emotions are the outcome of our thoughts. Imagine a day when you are feeling very good. If you were to analyse it, you would find that there is a positive thought at its root. Similarly, if you reflect on your thinking when you are feeling negative, you will find a negative thought pattern. In short, you become what you think.

So, if a person is good at building relationships, we may find that they carry the emotion of love or empathy towards others at a deeper level. When you ask them relevant questions, you will find their thought process behind this. They are doing what they do mainly because they are consciously or subconsciously thinking about how to build relationships. This is happening all the time in their minds.

Values and Beliefs

Going deeper, our thought process depends on our beliefs and value system. In the above example, the person carries such thoughts because, at a deeper level, he values people and believes that in order to achieve higher results one should value people and build lifelong relationships.

Another coaching client of mine was quite good at building relationships with everyone, but he was matter-of-fact and with senior colleagues. He was very professional and respectful, but could never build a strong rapport with senior leaders. When we discussed this in detail, he identified that this stemmed from his belief that one should respect elders while also maintaining a distance from them. This was probably based on the relationship he shared with his father. Our beliefs and values are therefore the key driver for our thought process, our emotions, and hence our behaviour.

In the context of role modelling it is important to understand all these things about your role model. Returning now to my coaching client who asked the question about how he should go about modelling his friend who was very good at time management, I asked him to find out the secrets of his friend's good time management. What are his actions, emotions, thoughts, values, and beliefs in this context? I also shared the iceberg model with my client.

Following this, my client spent a few hours observing him and asking him several deeper and specific questions including:

- How do you manage your time effectively?
- How do you deal with the ad hoc things that come your way?
- How do you feel when you have several things to do?
- What are your thoughts when you are swamped with unfinished work?
- Describe your entire process of managing yourself.

As a result of shadowing his role model for few hours and interacting with him, my client had the following observations to make:

- His friend planned, in advance, the top five things he wanted to achieve the following week. He usually spent 15 minutes on this on Sunday evenings.
- Every evening after the day's work, without fail, he planned for the next day. His belief was that one should not go to bed without planning the next day's work.
- He prioritised the next day's tasks into three categories. He always started the day by taking up the most difficult thing first.
- He placed high value on his own time and that of others too.
- He was firm in saying 'no' to unimportant things which could be time stealers.
- He believed that 'time management is self-management', and 'self-management is imperative for success'.

These were an eye opener for my client. He not only observed certain actions that his friend was taking, he was also able to understand his friend's thoughts, beliefs, and values behind those actions.

The mere realisation that one's beliefs and values drive one's outcomes was the turning point. My client was able to reflect on his actions, thoughts, beliefs, and values, and was able to make appropriate changes. Over 30 days of conscious self-observation and practice, my client was able to turn around his time management techniques. He identified his problem as not being able to say no to unimportant things. He realised that he had a belief that saying no was not a good thing and one should never refuse others.

In this manner, one can role model others by studying them, and having meaningful and deeper interactions with them.

Behaving as If You Are Already There

Another powerful step in this journey is believing that one is already there. I had a bank account in a multinational bank. I used to go there quite often, and was greeted and assisted by a young man who was very bright and cheerful. For a long time, I thought that he was the bank manager as he was well-dressed, confident, and cheerful, and knew exactly how to help customers. After some time, I was told that he was not the manager, but an intern at the bank. I knew very soon that this person would become a manager as he was already behaving like one. A year later, I went to another bank and there I saw the same young man who was now working as a manager.

The key to this young man's fast growth was his attitude. He always behaved as if he was already there. He dressed like a manager even though he was an intern. He talked like a manager, walked like a manager, and, most importantly, he had the body posture and body language of someone who was in a responsible position. It has been observed that if you start behaving like someone who is already there, very soon, you will reach there.

Our emotional state is also dependent on our body posture. For example, if we rest our head on our hand for some time, very soon we will start getting depressive thoughts. If you stand with your spine erect and carry a smile on your face, you will find that you will very soon feel confident and in control. Our physiology plays a very significant role in this. A good amount of research has been conducted in this space.[1] In cricket and other sports, modelling of body posture and body language is very prevalent and highly recommended.

Carrying the feeling that you are already there where you want to be, and behaving as if you are already there, helps you achieve faster results. During role modelling, make it a point to act like someone you are modelling. Pick up small habits and behaviours, and start practicing them till such time that they become your natural style.

Unique Ways of Learning

If one has the hunger to learn, one must reflect on the question, 'How do I learn best?' In other words, 'What is my preferred learning style?' Different people have different preferred learning styles; some learn by reading books, some learn by listening to audio or watching a video, some learn by attending lectures, whereas there are people who best learn by physically doing things.

Walter Burke Barbe and his colleagues have talked about three learning modalities popularly known as) VAK (visualising modality, auditory modality, kinesthetic modality). Neil Fleming added the read/write modality to it and called it VARK. These concepts can be utilised by any learner to maximise their learning by focusing on a mode they prefer. There are several ways to identify one's own unique learning style. One of the easiest is to observe yourself—reflect on your day-to-day life and find out how you learn most of the time.

For effective role modelling, you will need to utilise all learning styles with the primary focus being on your most preferred learning style.

Role Modelling Using Neuro-Linguistic Programming (NLP)

According to Robert Dilts (1998), modelling procedures involve identifying the mental strategies ('neuro') a person uses by analysing that person's language patterns ('linguistic') and non-verbal responses. The results of this analysis are then used in step-by-step strategies or procedures ('programming') that may be used to transfer the skill to other people, or applied to other contexts.

Richard Bandler (2008, p. 59) talks about a very powerful technique called 'Steal a Skill'. It has the following steps:

1. Identify a person you would like to model. Identify one aspect of their behaviour that you like the most and want to replicate or emulate. Sit in a relaxed manner and observe the person. For example, if effectively/calmly dealing with an irate customer is the behaviour you wish to emulate, simply observe carefully how your role model deals with an irate customer.
2. When you have observed your role model's behaviour a couple of times, and are clear about what you saw, close your eyes, relax, and recreate the entire performance of your role model as a sequence of various actions in your mind. Do this a few times. This is the model of excellence. Just feel how it feels, hear what you hear, and see what you see through this model of excellence with the image of your role model in it.
3. After replaying that a couple of times, move aside the mental image of your role model and step inside. Imagine now that it is you who is able to see through the eyes of excellence, hear through the ears of excellence, and feel the feelings of excellence.
4. Run through the same sequence of actions but from within, noticing this time what your body feels as you do this. Repeat several times till you get a sense of familiarity.
5. Step out of your role model's body, with the intention of retaining as much of the skill as possible as you return to normal working consciousness.
6. Now, at the earliest possible opportunity, and thereafter at every possible opportunity, practise the skills learnt in a real scenario while noticing how this exercise improves your performance.
7. Repeat the entire exercise, combining it with real time practice you do, at least once a day for the first 21 days, then at least once a week as maintenance.

One of my coaching clients was rather shy about asking his debtors to pay back what was due to him. He decided to role model his father who was very assertive. When he used Richard Bandler's seven steps mentioned above for 21 days, he observed a huge shift in him. This methodology is especially helpful when a shift has to be brought about at the subconscious belief level.

What If Role Modelling Fails?

Several times, my clients come to me and say that role modelling is not working for them. They say that they have been shadowing their role model for a few months, but have still not gotten closer to their desired level of success. This is a very natural and very common problem.

Each time someone says this, I ask them: What is the belief that is driving their role model? What is their thinking? What actions is the role model taking?

Role modelling generally fails when the follower either has incorrect or insufficient answers to the above questions. In such cases, I ask them to go deeper into their role-modelling practice. I encourage them to ask more probing questions and observe their role model more closely. Nearly 95% of coachees come back with a better discovery and positive results. In the remaining cases, I ask them to change their role model and that works for them.

It also depends a lot on how badly the coachee wants to get there. Persistence and focus always pay.

Workplace Role Modelling

Several working professionals face many challenges at work, which perplex them and generate stress. For example, it could be a lack of ability to accomplish big results, stress from trying to survive competition in the corporate world or handling conflicting relationships or feeling low on confidence due to an inability to express views freely. The list is long. Role modelling is a very good solution in all these situations.

To make the best and most effective use of role modelling as a technique, I recommend the following simple steps for role modelling at workplace.

1. Identify your career goals, which are aligned to your life purpose.
2. Identify the areas you are good at in the context of achieving your career goals.

3. Identify the areas you are not good at in the context of achieving your career goals.
4. Identify someone who is good at that skill, quality, or behaviour that you need to learn.
5. Seek a meeting with your role model to convey that you would like to model some of their strengths, and seek a convenient time and their consent.
6. Have one-to-one meetings and observe your role model. Identify your role model's actions, emotions, thoughts, values, and beliefs through observation, and by asking pertinent questions.
7. Take actions to imbibe learning.

The last step is of high significance. No amount of research will help unless you are committed to taking action.

In my experience, the most common areas where role modelling in the workplace works are:

- Enhancing time management
- Delivering presentations and public speaking
- Leading and inspiring a team
- Managing and leading change
- Better work–life balance
- Acquiring assertive behaviour
- Handing difficult communication
- Dealing with difficult scenarios
- Handling conflict at work
- Keeping composure

The above list is merely indicative, not exhaustive. Role modelling can practically work in every skill and quality that one seeks to hone.

Conclusion

Role modelling is a very powerful tool that can bring forth a change in one's behaviour, be it learning a simple skill or bringing about a transformative change in one's beliefs. It is a simple process and anyone can understand and follow it. It, however, requires a positive attitude towards learning, clarity of focus, and persistent effort.

Based on my experience of having worked in this space in the Indian context for nearly two decades, I feel that role modelling is not a very well utilised or sufficiently recognised tool. It still requires a lot of clarity and acceptance from masses. In India, role modelling is akin to ideal worship. In most cases, films stars, politicians, and cricketers are considered role models, mainly due to their popularity. Instead of emulating their beliefs and values, people generally tend to ape their role models' outward actions and mannerisms, often to the extent of worshiping them. Role modelling is a tool and should be used as a tool. That can only happen if more and more people in this country realise its power and start practising it.

In the game of cricket, the bowler keeps throwing more and more difficult balls towards the batsman, who is expected to hit sixes and fours until he is out. Life too is like a game of cricket, we face newer and more difficult challenges every day. It is up to us as to how we react to it. Do we shrug the difficult things away thinking 'It's not my cup of tea', or do we take them head on and say, 'I am ready to learn'? The choice is completely ours and we can make a big difference to our lives if we can say, 'Yes, I am ready to learn'. In case of the latter, you will soon find your role model somewhere around you. All the best!

Note

1. For example, see Amy Cuddy's 'Power Pose' series.

References

Alcorn, R. (2010, January 21). Florence Chadwick and the fog. *Eternal Perspective Ministries—Resources*. Retrieved May 19, 2017, from http://www.epm.org/resources/2010/Jan/21/florence-chadwick-and-fog/.

Bandler, R. (2008). *Guide to trance-formation: How to harness the power of hypnosis to ignite effortless and lasting change*. Deerfield Beach, FL: Health Communications, Inc.

BrainyQuote. (2016). Ralph Waldo Emerson quotes. *BrainyQuote*. Retrieved June 25, 2017, from https://www.brainyquote.com/quotes/quotes/r/ralphwaldo163674.html.

Dilts, R. (1998). *Modeling with NLP*. Capitola, CA: Meta Communications.

Reps, P., & Senzaki, N. (Compilers). (1957). *Zen flesh, Zen bones: A collection of Zen and pre-Zen writings*. North Clarendon, VT: Tuttle Publishing.

7

Fostering Vision, Culture, and Accountability in Young Organisations Through Role Modelling

Timothy Franklyn

Introduction

Unique cultural and organisational challenges present in an early-stage start-up environment. These challenges are exacerbated when founders do not have prior experience of working in India. My own experience as a corporate lawyer, having worked in Singapore and Hong Kong prior to starting up a media company in Bengaluru, India will illustrate this increasingly common phenomenon. In this chapter, I will discuss three different approaches to role modelling that founders can use to overcome such challenges and achieve the objectives of the organisation.

Role modelling of vision: ensuring that the founder's vision is shared by every member of the organisation. This can align motivations and skills, help attract the right talent, and move the organisation towards its objectives. The focus of this approach will be on making correct

T. Franklyn (✉)
National School of Journalism (NSoJ),
Bengaluru, India
e-mail: timothy.franklyn@nsoj.in; timothy_franklyn@hotmail.com

S. Vidyasagar and P. Hatti (eds.), *Leadership and Role Modelling*,
Palgrave Studies in Leadership and Followership,
https://doi.org/10.1007/978-3-319-69056-8_7

hiring decisions to ensure that role modelling can thrive within the organisation.

Role modelling of culture: start-ups have the opportunity to create and establish their own culture. Role modelling can help embed positive values within the organisation. Role modelling of unhealthy values may result in baking in a poor culture for the organisation in the long run.

Role modelling of accountability: the freedom for founders to run and manage their own organisation should manifest in them role-modelling accountability. Founders should resist the temptation to use this freedom to exempt themselves from being accountable in terms of work ethic, timeliness, deliverables, and measurable results.

This chapter draws on the available research in the areas of role modelling and entrepreneurship, as well as the experience of three entrepreneurs in their mid-thirties from Bengaluru, in managing young organisations: (a) Arvind Singh of Furdo, a Bengaluru-based interior design start-up, (b) Raghava K. K., an internationally renowned artist who established Flipsicle, a technology start-up in New York, and (c) myself as a founder of the National School of Journalism, Bangalore. I have chosen to study and compare the experiences of these founders because of the diversity of the sectors and markets in which their companies operate despite the founders being similarly aged and growing up in the same town. This diversity shows that the principles discussed in this chapter hold true (for the most part) irrespective of the type of company or the sector in which it operates. Most importantly, all the persons I have chosen are growing emerging businesses as part of a new wave of entrepreneurship among young Indians.

The Importance of Hiring Well to Execute a Vision

A major feature of nascent businesses is the vision of the founder or founders. The founders' belief in this vision is in most cases the *raison d'être* of the business itself. For young businesses to be successful, it is critical that key hires in vital areas of the organisation are filled by persons who share, and buy into, this vision.

Start-ups have to handle the absence of established relationships, roles, and routines, such external and internal interconnections being critical resources of the firm (Pfeffer & Salancik, 1978). The lack of a business network and practices increases financial pressure at a time when new businesses have limited resources (Eisenhardt & Schoonhoven, 1990). Young businesses attempt to overcome the lack of resources, unestablished brand identity, and absence of a track record by providing services and interactions that are highly personalised, involved, and customised to the needs of customers or clients. An effective way to achieve this is to hire employees that perform their roles with the awareness of, and belief in, the founders' vision. It is this belief that enables employees to work long hours enthusiastically, in roles that are not clearly defined, and for less money than they would expect to receive in a traditional, established company.

As a natural corollary (for the very reasons mentioned above), employees who do not subscribe to the founders' vision but treat the role as just a 'job' for which they are paid a salary are unlikely to be productive or helpful in achieving the objectives of the organisation, leading to high employee dissatisfaction and frustration.

Role modelling can help employees in nascent businesses share and believe in the vision of the founders. There are three ways in which young organisations can create an environment that is conducive for role-modelling-based management to thrive. First, founders should identify the right attributes in the prospective hires in their candidate pool from which to choose critical resources. Second, founders should ascertain during the hiring process whether or not a rapport exists or can be developed between the founder (role model) and the candidate. Third, founders should make every effort to serve as living examples that will allow employees to thrive within the organisation and become role models themselves as they move on to the middle and late stages of their careers, thereby establishing a healthy culture in the workplace.

Identifying the Right Pool of Candidates to Hire: Human Capital and Career Stage

Making the right critical hires in a young organisation is important, as these persons usually help execute the vision of the founders, grow the organisation, and play an important role in establishing the culture of the organisation. If the objective of founders is to create successful organisations with a culture that reflects their own work ethic, creativity, integrity, and values it is of vital importance that key employees are hired from a pool of candidates with attributes that will make role modelling effective within the organisation.

Choose from a Pool of Highly Educated and Skilled Candidates

In Indian society, where feudal models of entrepreneurship persist, that is, employer–employee relationships mimic master–slave relationships, it is natural for young entrepreneurs to be sceptical of highly educated and skilled candidates. The need for entrepreneurs to be better skilled than potential employees is thought necessary to maintain a dominant position in the relationship.

However, there is a higher likelihood of role modelling being effective when persons with high levels of human capital, a combination of educational attainment, intelligence, knowledge, and skills that a person possesses, are hired. This premise is based on the notion of absorptive capacity (Cohen & Levinthal, 1990). The ability to value, interpret, and apply (external) knowledge (that is, role model influences) requires a certain level of knowledge and skills. In addition, more highly educated individuals may have more ambitious goals and may therefore be in greater need of successful examples or support. More highly educated people are also better able to absorb information provided by role models.

On the other hand, social learning theory postulates that there should be opportunities to learn from a role model (through example or support) and this is more likely when the role model is more highly qualified than the role model 'user': that is, there is potential learning in dissimilarity. A role model often has a higher hierarchical position (Kram & Isabella, 1985; Shapiro, Haseltine, & Row, 1978). Bandura and Walters (1963) argue that, to be imitated, a role model needs to be socially effective or successful.

I believe that both these concepts reinforce my view that it is important to hire persons with high human capital. It is possible (and likely) that role models can win the respect of the 'user' by being socially effective and successful without having to be better qualified or proficient in terms of specialist skills or knowledge. At any rate, research shows that most business founders have distinct characteristics that set them apart from the rest. Especially during the start-up phase entrepreneurs are regarded as different from the normal population. They are endowed with an inborn intuition, self-esteem, risk taking, and need for achievements which are reflected in their attitudes. Anticipating the future and finding opportunities are key variables in accomplishing entrepreneurial goals (Cunningham & Lischeron, 1991). Start-up founders naturally will find themselves in a superior hierarchical position without having to compete with their employees on human capital terms.

In my experience as a corporate lawyer early on in my career, I developed an interest in international trade sanctions, which was domain knowledge that the partner (role model) in the law firm where I worked did not possess. The fact that he encouraged my interest in this area of law and promoted it within the firm and to external clients in no way diminished my respect for him. Contrarily, I felt valued by my role model and inspired to achieve more for the firm and learn from him various managerial and business development skills.

Arvind Singh notes: 'It is important for the hire to be better skilled than the role model in his chosen area of specialisation.' This works on multiple levels. First, the employee is able to fully express his skills without having to worry about upstaging her role model and risk jeopardising the traditional employer–employee relationship. Second, it frees the entrepreneur in using his time to grow the business rather than in supervising and micromanaging the hire. Third, the role model can build a respectful relationship with the employee that focuses on role-modelling vision and values, rather than skills.

Entrepreneurs must however bear in mind that high human capital can serve as a substitute for the support of a role model. Individuals with higher levels of human capital may be less likely to have entrepreneurial role models as a source of inspiration, learning, and self-efficacy (Gimeno, Folta, Cooper, & Woo, 1997; Hamilton, 2000; Hartog, Van Praag, & Van der Sluis, 2010; Parker & Van Praag, 2006; Stuart & Abetti, 1990; Van Praag, van Witteloostuijn, & Van der Sluis, 2009). It is therefore important, particularly when hiring persons with high human capital, to look for personality traits such as open-mindedness, and the willingness to listen, learn, and evaluate multiple viewpoints.

Raghava K. K., who is a father of four young children, explains: 'There is an intersection between running a family and a business. There is a certain order, level of trust, and leadership required in both roles. In parenting, you can tell your children whatever you want, but they learn most from observing your actions. So, if you tell them to be honest and truthful, but ask them to answer your phone and say you are not there, they will learn from that! What this means for business is that role modelling is very effective because your employees will learn from your actions. But role modelling cannot be a job—it fails when it is contrived. Projecting values or traits that you do not possess destroys the very premise of role modelling. For role modelling to work, you need to be authentic and that is tough, particularly in transactional environments, where showing vulnerability can be construed to be a weakness.'

This is where hiring employees with high human capital can make a difference. These candidates may be inclined and able to learn from authentic role models while making allowance for the models' vulnerabilities. Raghava recalls a conversation with Bill Gates, in which the latter remarked, 'I am not the smartest person in the room, but I am smart because I surround myself with people who are smarter than me.' Good leadership is not about delegating skills down the chain because of a bandwidth problem, and so role modelling as a management model in start-ups should be less about role-modelling skills and more about role modelling values and vision.

Choose from a Pool of Candidates in the Early Stage of Their Careers

Recruiting for a start-up from a pool of persons who are in the early stage of their careers is important from a role-modelling perspective because early-stage professionals have a desire to learn two primary things from their role models: (a) how to perform tasks competently and professionally and (b) how to fit into their professional role both by matching the characteristics of the organisational culture and by earning the respect of their colleagues (Gibson, 2003).

Early-stage employees are also more likely to construe their role models as positive and as possessing global attributes, while middle-stage and late-stage employees are more likely to construe role models as negative and construe specific attributes and skills. Global attributes include a range of attributes in 'one package', including personal traits ('integrity, care about people'), and organisationally relevant skills ('terrific with clients', 'interpersonal skills', 'process skills'). The global dimension indicates that early career–stage hires are open to several possible inputs from a role model, from the professional to the personal (Gibson, 2003). Construing positive role model attributes includes a sense of perceived or desired similarity, a sense that the role model offered relevant task or skill expertise, and a sense that the role model could help the observer develop as a person. Early career–stage hires are more likely to look to role models and see their actions as a goal or as an aspiration. On the other hand, middle and late career–stage employees are more likely to construe negative role model attributes, that is, attributes of a role model that are sought out as examples of how *not* to behave in a particular context (Gibson, 2003).

When I was on the recruitment committee of the Hong Kong office of DLA Piper, one of the largest law firms in the world, I interviewed several job applicants (recent graduates and experienced lawyers). International law firms have robust procedures that rely primarily on hiring young lawyers straight out of law school as trainees for a couple of years before hiring them as associates. Very seldom are junior associates hired from among those who did not complete their training at the same law firm. This is for very good reason. Trainees in our firm who went on to join us as associates were more likely to contribute effectively to the team (although they may never have worked with that particular team during their training period in the firm) than extremely competent junior (or even mid-level) associates who may have joined us from a different firm.

The orientation to positive attributes by early-stage hires therefore provides for a work environment in a young organisation that makes role modelling of vision and culture effective. In my own experience, I have found that early-stage hires are better able to grasp my approach to innovative thinking and dynamic work outcomes to produce results that have surpassed expectations. On the other hand, employees in the middle stage of their career require more persuasion and convincing to embark on a particular course of action, which can be frustrating for persons—like me—who adopt a democratic style of leadership and decision-making as much as possible.

Race and Gender Similarities Between the Employee and Entrepreneur

Based on role identification theory and the role model function of increasing self-efficacy, some degree of similarity between the observer and the role model (at least in the perception of the observer) is to be expected, even if the role model occupies a (more) desirable position. Without such similarity, it is difficult for the entrepreneur to perceive the behaviour of the role model as compatible with the own (perceived) behavioural opportunities, that is, 'I can do anything (s) he can'. Empirical evidence, for example, suggests that individuals and their role models tend to be similar in terms of gender and race (Hernandez, 1995; Maccoby & Jacklin, 1974; Ruef, Aldrich, & Carter, 2003). In general, homophily, that is the tendency of individuals to associate and bond with similar others, guides many relationships (McPherson, Smith-Lovin, & Cook, 2001). In addition, ethnic homophily has been identified in the workplace (Reskin, McBrier, & Kmec, 1999).

This presents an interesting challenge for entrepreneurs who have spent much of their professional careers living in other countries and have gone back to their home country to launch their entrepreneurial pursuit. My experience as a corporate lawyer who studied in England, and worked in Singapore and Hong Kong for 10 years before starting up a media company and journalism school in Bengaluru, India, illustrates this increasingly common phenomenon. On the other hand, Raghava started up a social media technology company in New York.

My experience after moving back to India is that I miss the opportunities to socialise with colleagues after work. I believe that I have learned much professionally and developed as a person as a result of interacting with my role models during my career as an international corporate finance lawyer. I learnt most from them while watching a sports game together or socialising with the team after work. In India, I miss the ability for individuals within the organisation across functions and roles to naturally socialise outside of work. In India, the norm is for employees (regardless of gender) to socialise with each other separately and founders (or employers) to do so separately—other than in formal gatherings that lead to awkward exchanges of social niceties. There is an inherent ability in Indians to establish classes of people in any social context—perhaps this is somehow related to India's caste system. The result of this phenomenon is that it is difficult to develop the role model relationship outside the professional context. This makes role modelling in India less than optimal for this reason.

Furthermore, social and cultural realities in India make it difficult for cross-gender mentoring and role modelling, particularly when it comes to learning skills, attitudes, and behaviours outside work in a social setting. However, there is an ironic upside to the cultural realities of working in India: because there tends to be less socialising between role models and followers in India in general, the benefits of role modelling tend to be denied to both genders in equal measure!

The hindrances to cross-gender mentoring and role modelling are somewhat reduced in Western cultures. Nonetheless gender affinities still tend to be formed because of social conditioning. I have found that it is much more frequent for role models to have a close one-on-one social relationship with their followers of the same sex, through activities such as lunches, dinners, sports activities, and drinks, than with someone of the opposite sex. This results in distorted role-modelling outcomes in the workplace, where persons whose role models are of the same sex benefit more than their peers of the opposite sex.

As a hiring matter, though, do I tend to be more favourably disposed to hire persons with a Western outlook, someone with whom I share similarities? People from Bengaluru generally tend to be more cosmopolitan than most people from most other Indian cities, but even so, the answer is clearly, yes. This is because I can more readily develop a rapport with them. In the following paragraphs, I explain why 'rapport' is a key component of successfully implementing role modelling as an approach to managing a young organisation.

Having identified the talent pool to hire from, let us now explore ways in which founders can make the correct hiring decision from among this pool.

Assessing and Building Rapport During the Hiring Process

It is vital during the hiring process that founders spend sufficient time with a candidate to assess the receptiveness of the candidate to learning new tasks and skills, particularly those that the founder possesses. Social learning theory (Bandura, 1977) suggests that individuals are attracted to role models who can help them in developing themselves further by learning new tasks and skills (Gibson, 2004). This attraction or rapport is a crucial indicator of the success that the founder will have in role modelling his vision in the prospective employee.

Rapport is also a good indicator of role identification as a response to an individual's belief that the characteristics of the model are close to her own motives and character (Kagan, 1958) and that this model plays a desirable—often central—social role or occupies an attractive position (Bell, 1970). Role identification may result in the formation or adaptation of an individual's preferences (Witt, 1991) or in imitative behaviour if this is expected to be rewarding (Kagan, 1958). It may provide someone with the motivation and inspiration to choose a particular direction, activity, or career path (Krumboltz, Mitchell, & Jones, 1976). People are assumed to learn in a social context through the observation of others with whom they can identify and who perform well in an area in which they, themselves, also wish to be involved or in which they want to excel, that is, learning by example (or modelling) (Bosma, Hessels, Schutjens, van Praag, & Verheul, 2012). The identification of, and comparison with, role models may help individuals define their self-concept or sense of self (Akerlof & Kranton, 2000) and enhance their self-efficacy to engage in a certain occupation (De Clercq & Arenius, 2006; Gibson, 2004; Lockwood & Kunda, 1997).

Developing rapport is also essential from the candidate's perspective to get a clear picture of the role model's personality. The first characteristic of an effective role model is consideration (Jago, 1982). This refers to the model's ability to communicate with the observer, who will up-value their role model if they are in agreement with him. The role model needs to consider that each group member responds differently to him. This consideration is about mutual trust, respect, and a rapport between the role model and his team (Fleishman, Harris, & Burtt, 1955). During the interview process, it is important for the candidate to assess whether or not the prospective employer can also be an effective leader and role model.

Since the role of positive entrepreneurial examples is important for enhancing entrepreneurial activity (Fornahl, 2003, p. 50), all the factors above associated with establishing rapport are indicators of the likelihood of the founders' success in role modelling the vision to a prospective employee. As a practical matter, founders may need to acknowledge that if there is little or no rapport established at the end of the hiring process, the likelihood of the candidate being motivated to buy into the founders' vision will be somewhat limited. Not being able to successfully role model the vision of the organisation can have a direct bearing on the candidate's ability to undertake entrepreneurial activity on behalf of the organisation. Over the last three years, I have hired persons with whom I developed good rapport during the hiring process, as well as those with whom I may have failed to develop a good rapport but whose skills and knowledge bases were strong.

I find that even after working for years together it is very difficult to build rapport with those with whom no rapport was established at the end of the hiring process. When I look back on my life as a lawyer who worked at two major global law firms, Allen & Overy and DLA Piper, I can distinctly remember not making a connection with some people during my own job interviews, and true enough, those connections have yet to be made more than a decade later! On the contrary, partners in both firms with whom a good rapport was built during the hiring process were solid role models for me professionally, and remain close friends today.

Arvind Singh says: 'You can have the grandest vision and the perfect plan to translate vision into actionable steps, but if an employee charged with implementing any critical portion of the vision does not believe in the vision, then it's a hiring mistake. So, as a founder, I am better off waiting to hire someone with the right skills who can be excited about the vision than to hire someone who is disinterested in the vision with the hope that they will somehow deliver once we start working together. Hiring mistakes can be detrimental to the growth of a start-up because it can interfere structurally in the business plans of the founders, who may begin to question the viability of the business plan, when the real problem might be simply a hiring mistake.'

I agree with Arvind, and find that persons who are excited by the vision during the hiring process are the ones with whom a natural rapport develops. I have found no discernible differences between male and female candidates in terms of their enthusiasm to embrace the vision of the organisation during the hiring process. But it is worth noting that I find female candidates to be more committed to implementing that vision than their male counterparts—this finding is purely anecdotal and requires further study.

Role Modelling in Start-Up Organisations

You have identified the right talent pool, and have hired the right candidate. Now begins the real work of role modelling. And it is completely up to the founders (role models) to either create a great culture within the organisation or poor culture (as we will see with a recent example).

How the motivation of the lead is linked to that of the employee's is demonstrated in the study by Tierney, Farmer, and Graen (1999). Data from this study shows that the employee's motivation depends highly on the leader's drive, because when the leader's intrinsic motivation is low, employee intrinsic motivation is irrelevant.

Since start-ups move through several stages quite frequently and witness unexpected situations, a situational leadership style is most commonly employed in start-ups. Sometimes, leaders need to make a decision very quickly without substantial knowledge or background, requiring on-the-feet thinking. These situations demand spontaneous and impulsive advice. The situational leadership concept holds that different situations require different approaches of leadership. It states that there is no single all-purpose leadership style. The person in charge needs to assess the situation and adapt his skills, techniques, and decisions according to that. This concept attempts to match the leadership style to the conditions the situation requires (Hall, 2007). The situational approach helps managers to diagnose the demands of their individual situations. It is built on an intersection of the amount of direction a leader gives, the amount of socio-emotional support a leader offers, and the readiness level that followers exhibit on a specific task (Hersey, Blanchard, & Natemeyer, 1979).

Role-Modelling Vision

According to Gibson (2004, p. 136), 'The term "role model" draws on two prominent theoretical constructs: the concept of role and the tendency of individuals to identify with other people ... and the concept of modelling, the psychological matching of cognitive skills and patterns of behavior between a person and an observing individual.' He summarises the various functions that role models may fulfil and argues that the importance of role models lies in three interrelated functions: to provide learning, to provide motivation and inspiration, and to help individuals define their self-concept (Gibson, 2004, p. 149). Assessing the influence of role models on students' academic and vocational decisions, Nauta and Kokaly (2001) add a support component, arguing that role models not only provide individuals with inspiration and modelling, but also with support and guidance.

When employees endorse and internalise the leader's way of thinking they become intrinsically motivated and personally engaged in their work (Tierney et al., 1999). The more the leader demonstrates and exemplifies a certain behaviour, the more it will affirm for employees that this is expected. Personally engaged employees are essential as they stand behind the company's activities (Bruggeman, 2014).

There are some 'visions' that on the face of it appear to be more motivational than others. For instance, it may appear that launching a journalism school with a vision to 'train journalists who care deeply about justice and democracy' will be more motivational than a technology start-up with a vision to make it easy for people to design the interiors of their new home to world-class standards. But this is not true. It goes back to the first step in the process, which is hiring a person with the potential to share the vision and identify with the founder. In the example above, it may in fact be relatively easier to identify a skilled young person in India who cares passionately about design and furniture than about democracy and justice!

In his organisations, Raghava designs a Myth, Art and Ritual (MAR) structure. 'Myth' is the story, the vision, the philosophy, or the concept, 'Art' is the reinforcement of a myth, and 'Ritual' is the participation in the myth through art. Raghava reiterates 'Everyone in the organisation consciously realises that their work is effectively participating in the myth (or vision) of the organisation. The process of modelling is the art, the experience of modelling is the ritual, and the values on which you are modelling is the myth or the vision.'

It is therefore essential for role models to build channels of communication keeping their vision in mind. Here the focus lies on completing tasks, meeting deadlines, and establishing relationships among employees. The role model clearly defines what he expects, plans ahead, assigns tasks, and stresses on the throughput of projects (Fleishman et al., 1955). The study by Jago (1982) sees a correlation between consideration and performance. He says that increased performance is caused by a higher level of consideration, sensitivity, and support. As a conclusion, the role model who is low in consideration and low in launching a structure has a lesser supply of rewards (Evans, 1970).

Motivating the observer through role modelling the founders' vision is predicated on providing employees other motivating factors that play an important part in the role-modelling process. For most founders, one major motivating factor for the business to succeed is the fact that the founder has an ownership interest in the enterprise. It follows logically that founders cannot expect to have employees be motivated to achieve the vision of the organisation without them also having some sense of ownership in the business.

Arvind Singh believes that creating an equity pool for key employees is important to establish at the very outset. Whether or not the business eventually succeeds, employees participating in the equity pool will work with the knowledge that their interests and those of the founders are aligned to achieve success for the organisation. Employees will also be more empathetic to financial constraints that young companies may face, and may be willing to work at lower wages to achieve the vision of the founders with the knowledge that (a) the founders and employees win or lose together and (b) they will be rewarded as the organisation grows.

It is unreasonable to expect that employees work tirelessly and passionately to achieve the founders' vision without any promise of benefitting monetarily from the growth of the organisation. More importantly, participating in an equity pool makes employees feel that they share in the ownership of the organisation, a key unifier that allows them to be more receptive to follow the example of their entrepreneur role models.

Role-Modelling Culture

In general, entrepreneurs are described as being different from other people. They have a certain way of thinking that is a prerequisite for starting up. Ireland, Hitt, and Sirmon (2003) discuss an entrepreneurial mind-set that is both an individualistic and collective phenomenon. This mind-set is constantly faced with uncertainty while keeping the growth-oriented perspective. This attitude is essential for identifying and exploiting new prospects. Nearly all studies published in literature agree on certain personality traits for entrepreneurs. The most common characteristics identified in these studies are achievement motivation, risk-taking, and locus of control (Rauch & Frese, 2000).

People who follow entrepreneurial principles create a sort of a culture where 'new ideas and creativity are expected, risk taking is encouraged, failure is tolerated, learning is promoted, and continuous change is viewed as a conveyor of opportunities' (Ireland et al., 2003, p. 971). Role modelling in a start-up therefore moves very quickly from leadership to establishing the culture of an organisation. Establishing the right culture at an organisation is important at the early stage of its development. The role model may move on but the culture can live on in perpetuity within the organisation.

On this point, it is instructive to view the recent friction between founders of the 36-year-old Bangalore-based software giant, Infosys Limited, and its current management team (ETMarkets.com, 2017). Without going into the merits of the issue, the main issue at hand is the perception among the founders (who are currently in an executive or management position) that the leadership team (in early 2017) had departed from the values and culture of Infosys that were role modelled by its founders. One of the founders disagreed with the manner in which principles governing the CEO's compensation—as role modelled by him three decades ago—were set aside in favour of extraordinarily high compensation in recent times. One could even argue that the erosion of more than five billion US dollars in market value of Infosys stock[1] (Korgaonkar, 2017) boils down to a cultural issue with little to do with the actual financial performance of the company.

That is the power of culture, and the role of the founders in establishing this culture. The call for the new CEO role to be appointed from within Infosys and not be filled by an outsider supports the view that changing the culture of an organisation late in its development is not easy and can even be destructive to an organisation.

It is therefore critical that the founders' role model the right values during the early stages of an organisation. This can however prove to be a challenge for founders in start-up organisations, since they mostly are inexperienced and without formal training in management and human resource development (Bruggemann, 2014). Put simply, 'entrepreneurs tend to be more intuitive and less analytic than non-entrepreneurs' (Armstrong & Hird, 2009, p. 419). Being a good role model under these circumstances requires discipline, perseverance, and maturity.

Failure to pay attention can lead to unaccountability on the part of the founders in decision-making and behavioural patterns, which can lead to poor work culture setting into the organisation.

Role-Modelling Accountability

Anecdotal experience and research show that it is desirable for young organisations to choose employees critical to the business from a pool of proficient candidates that are in the early stages of their own careers so that such organisations can maximise the benefits of role modelling. The natural consequence of this strategy is that as these early-stage high performers grow into their careers, they likely will have absorbed the values and culture of their role models, which will result in them assuming the role model position for new hires entering the organisation. This in turn can, within a few years, establish the culture of the organisation.

The adverse effects of poor role modelling can be extremely damaging to the long-term culture of an organisation. This has been obvious among some successful start-ups in California—Uber being the most recent example—where an undesirable workplace culture was established and became pervasive, resulting in several top executives leaving the company. The BBC reports that since being founded in 2009, Uber has gained a reputation as a company that espouses Silicon Valley's so-called 'bro' culture of male-dominated, macho work environments, and has been the subject of allegations of sexual harassment and misogyny (Lee, 2017). This phenomenon is consistent with evidence of gender homophily that has been found in various contexts, such as large organisations (Kalleberg, Knoke, Marsden, & Spaeth, 1996), networks (Ibarra, 1997), and voluntary organisations (McPherson & Smith-Lovin, 1987).

To elaborate: In 2017, Uber was subject to an investigation headed by former United States Attorney General, Eric Holder (BBC, 2017). Mr. Holder is reported to have recommended introducing more control on spending, human resources, and other areas where executives led by Travis Kalanick, founder and former CEO, have had an unusual degree of autonomy for a company of Uber's size (Johnston, 2017). That this kind of culture is pervasive at Uber and other Silicon Valley start-ups demonstrates the effect that poor role models can have on corporate behemoths that were recent start-ups. When Uber board member Arianna Huffington said that Mr. Kalanick needed to change his leadership style from that of a 'scrappy entrepreneur' to be more like a 'leader of a major global company', it was a stark warning of the kind of influential role model Mr. Kalanick had been to Uber (Johnston, 2017).

The starting point of good role modelling in a young organisation is the founder. The founder herself is the product of her surroundings and her values are a reflection of the role models that influenced her. My experiences of interacting with my own role models define the person I am and the principles I adhere to. My role models at home (parents), in school and college (teachers and seniors), at the sports field (coaches and captains), in the choir (the conductor), at the law firm, and in the person of Jesus of Nazareth, have all had a significant influence in the values I model within my organisation.

So, when do you start role modelling? You start from the very first time someone looks up to you as an example: perhaps in relation to your younger sibling when you were five. It is not a skill that can be learned at the time you establish your first company or when you become CEO of a 30-billion-dollar company.

As the vision of the founder and role model grows the start-up into a large corporation, a founder's all-round character traits have tremendous potential to influence. Founders must be responsible to ensure that their actions reflect good values all round, which can translate into establishment of a good culture in the organisation.

Note

1. The relentless campaign by Narayana Murthy, one of the founders of Infosys, against the perceived lapses in corporate governance and high executive compensation led to the resignation of the CEO of Infosys, Vishal Sikka, and there was a sudden and steep drop in the share price of Infosys. The full text of Mr. Murthy's letter to the media may be found online at http://www.reuters.com/article/infosys-murthy-letter/full-text-of-infosys-founder-narayana-murthys-letter-to-the-media-

idUSL3N1HB1WC and http://www.hindustantimes.com/business-news/infosys-stocks-fall-over-6-on-vishal-sikka-s-resignation/story-htTOD-t8j3HQwoy4eLgrAVM.html.

References

Akerlof, G. A., & Kranton, R. E. (2000). Economics and identity. *The Quarterly Journal of Economics, 115*(3), 715–753.

Armstrong, S. J., & Hird, A. (2009). Cognitive style and entrepreneurial drive of new and mature business owner-managers. *Journal of Business and Psychology, 24*(4), 419–430.

Bandura, A. (1977). *Social learning theory*. Englewood Cliffs, NJ: Prentice-Hall.

Bandura, A., & Walters, R. (1963). *Social learning and personality development.* New York: Holt, Rinehart, and Winston.

BBC. (2017, June 12). Uber chief Travis Kalanick may face bumpy ride. *BBC News—Business*. Retrieved on 17 September 2017 from http://www.bbc.com/news/business-40242538.

Bell, A. (1970). Role modelship and interaction in adolescence and young adulthood. *Developmental Psychology, 2*(1), 123–128.

Bosma, N., Hessels, J., Schutjens, V., van Praag, M., & Verheul, I. (2012). Entrepreneurship and role models. *Journal of Economic Psychology, 33*(2), 410–424. https://doi.org/10.1016/j.joep.2011.03.004.

Bruggemann, H. (2014). *Entrepreneurial leadership styles: A comparative study between startups and mature firms.* Retrieved on 13 June 2017 from http://essay.utwente.nl/65376/1/Br%C3%BCggemann_BA_faculty%20of%20Management%20and%20Governance.pdf.

Cohen, W. M., & Levinthal, D. A. (1990). Absorptive capacity: A new perspective on learning and innovation. *Administrative Science Quarterly, 35*(1), 128–152.

Cunningham, J. B., & Lischeron, J. (1991). Defining entrepreneurship. *Journal of Small Business Management, 29*(1), 45–61.

De Clercq, D., & Arenius, P. (2006). The role of knowledge in business start-up activity. *International Small Business Journal, 24*(4), 339–358.

Eisenhardt, K. M., & Schoonhoven, C. B. (1990). Organisational growth: Linking founding team, strategy, environment, and growth among US semiconductor ventures, 1978–1988. *Administrative Science Quarterly, 35*(3), 504–529.

ETMarkets.com. (2017, August 18). Why Vishal Sikka quit as Infosys MD: Full text of his resignation letter. *The Economic Times*. Retrieved on 16 September 2017 from http://economictimes.indiatimes.com/articleshow/60113647.cms?utm_source=contentofinterest&utm_medium=text&utm_campaign=cppst.

Evans, M. G. (1970). The effects of supervisory behavior on the path-goal relationship. *Organisational Behavior and Human Performance, 5*(3), 277–298.

Fleishman, E. A., Harris, E. F., & Burtt, H. E. (1955). *Leadership and supervision in industry: An evaluation of a supervisory training program*. Columbus, OH: The Ohio State University.

Fornahl, D. (2003). Entrepreneurial activities in a regional context. In D. Fornahl & T. Brenner (Eds.), *Cooperation, networks and institutions in regional innovation systems* (pp. 38–57). Cheltenham: Edward Elgar.

Gibson, D. E. (2003). Developing the professional self-concept: Role model construals in early, middle, and late career stages. *Organisation Science, 14*(5), 591–610.

Gibson, D. E. (2004). Role models in career development: New directions for theory and research. *Journal of Vocational Behavior, 65*(1), 134–156.

Gimeno, J., Folta, T., Cooper, A., & Woo, C. (1997). Survival of the fittest? Entrepreneurial human capital and the persistence of underperforming firms. *Administrative Science Quarterly, 42*(4), 750–783.

Hall, A. (2007). *Entrepreneurial leadership: A profile of Herb Kelleher and South West Airlines*. Completed in Partial fulfilment of the Requirements for OM 8107—Entrepreneurial Leader as Pioneer. Minneapolis, MN: Capella University.

Hamilton, B. (2000). Does entrepreneurship pay? An empirical analysis of the returns to self-employment. *Journal of Political Economy, 108*(3), 604–631.

Hartog, J., Van Praag, M., & Van der Sluis, J. (2010). If you are so smart, why aren't you an entrepreneur? Returns to cognitive and social ability: Entrepreneurs versus employees. *Journal of Economics and Management Strategy, 19*(4), 947–989. https://doi.org/10.1111/j.1530-9134.2010.00274.x.

Hernandez, A. E. (1995). Do role models influence self efficacy and aspirations in Mexican American at-risk females? *Hispanic Journal of Behavioral Sciences, 17*(2), 256–263.

Hersey, P., Blanchard, K. H., & Natemeyer, W. E. (1979). Situational leadership, perception, and the impact of power. *Group & Organisation Management, 4*(4), 418–428.

Ibarra, H. (1997). Paving an alternative route: Gender differences in managerial networks. *Social Psychology Quarterly, 60*(1), 91–102.

Ireland, D., Hitt, M. A., & Sirmon, D. G. (2003). A model of strategic entrepreneurship: The construct and its dimensions. *Journal of Management, 29*(6), 963–989. https://doi.org/10.1016/S0149-2063_03_00086-2.

Jago, A. G. (1982). Leadership: Perspectives in theory and research. *Management Science, 28*(3), 315–336.

Johnston, C. (2017, June 12). Uber loses another top executive Emil Michael. *BBC News—Business*. Retrieved on 16 September 2017 from http://www.bbc.com/news/business-40254388.

Kagan, J. (1958). The concept of identification. *Psychological Review, 65*(5), 296–305.

Kalleberg, A. L., Knoke, D., Marsden, P. V., & Spaeth, J. L. (1996). *Organizations in America: Analyzing their structures and human resource practices*. Thousand Oaks, CA: SAGE.

Korgaonkar, D. (2017, August 21). Infosys loses Rs 34,000 crore in market-cap in two days. *Business Standard*. Retrieved on 16 September 2017 from http://www.business-standard.com/article/markets/infosys-out-of-top-10-lost-rs-34-500-crore-of-market-cap-in-two-days-117082100514_1.html.

Kram, K. E., & Isabella, L. (1985). Mentoring alternatives: The role of peer relationships in career development. *Academy of Management Journal, 28*(1), 110–132. https://doi.org/10.2307/256064.

Krumboltz, J. D., Mitchell, A. M., & Jones, G. B. (1976). A social learning theory of career selection. *The Counseling Psychologist, 6*(1), 71–80.

Lee, D. (2017, February 20). Uber investigates 'abhorrent' sexism claims. *BBC News—Technology*. Retrieved on 23 August 2017 from http://www.bbc.com/news/technology-39024445.

Lockwood, P., & Kunda, Z. (1997). Superstars and me: Predicting the impact of role models on the self. *Journal of Personality and Social Psychology, 73*, 91–103.

Maccoby, E. E., & Jacklin, C. N. (1974). *The psychology of sex differences*. Stanford, CA: Stanford University Press.

McPherson, M., & Smith-Lovin, L. (1987). Homophily in voluntary organisations: Status distance and the composition of face-to-face groups. *American Sociological Review, 52*(3), 370–379.

McPherson, M., Smith-Lovin, L., & Cook, J. (2001). Birds of a feather: Homophily in social networks. *Annual Review of Sociology, 27*, 415–444. https://doi.org/10.1146/annurev.soc.27.1.415.

Nauta, M., & Kokaly, M. (2001). Assessing role model influences on students' academic and vocational decisions. *Journal of Career Assessment, 9*(1), 81–99.

Parker, S. C., & Van Praag, M. (2006). Schooling, capital constraints and entrepreneurial performance: The endogenous triangle. *Journal of Business and Economic Statistics, 24*(4), 416–431.

Pfeffer, J., & Salancik, G. R. (1978). *The external control of organisations: A resource dependence perspective*. New York: Harper and Row.

Rauch, A., & Frese, M. (2000). Psychological approaches to entrepreneurial success: A general model and an overview of findings. *International Review of Industrial and Organisational Psychology, 15,* 101–142.

Reskin, B. F., McBrier, D. B., & Kmec, J. A. (1999). The determinants of workplace sex and race composition. *Annual Review of Sociology, 25,* 335–361. https://doi.org/10.1146/annurev.soc.25.1.335.

Ruef, M., Aldrich, H. E., & Carter, N. M. (2003). The structure of founding teams: Homophily, strong ties, and isolation among U.S. entrepreneurs. *American Sociological Review, 68*(2), 195–222.

Shapiro, E. C., Haseltine, F. P., & Rowe, M. P. (1978). Moving up: Role models, mentors, and the 'patron system'. *Sloan Management Review, 19*(3), 51–58.

Stuart, R. W., & Abetti, P. A. (1990). The impact of entrepreneurial and management experience on early performance. *Journal of Business Venturing, 5*(3), 151–162.

Tierney, P., Farmer, S. M., & Graen, G. B. (1999). An examination of leadership and employee creativity: The relevance of traits and relationships. *Personnel Psychology, 52*(3), 591–620.

Van Praag, M., van Witteloostuijn, A., & Van der Sluis, J. (2009). *Returns for entrepreneurs versus employees: The effect of education and personal control on the relative performance of entrepreneurs*. Tinbergen Institute Discussion Paper TI 2009-111/3. Amsterdam: Tinbergen Institute Amsterdam. Retrieved on 12 June 2017 from https://papers.tinbergen.nl/09111.pdf.

Witt, U. (1991). Economics, sociobiology, and behavioral psychology on preferences. *Journal of Economic Psychology, 12*(4), 557–573. https://doi.org/10.1016/0167-4870(91)90001-A.

8

Being and Following Role Models

Raju Ramachandran, T. S. Sridhar, and Sudarshan Iyengar

Finding Role Models Inside and Outside the Legal Profession

Raju Ramachandran

I wonder if it is a mere coincidence that I am writing this on the very day that one of my role models has passed away. T. R. Andhyarujina was

R. Ramachandran (✉)
Supreme Court of India, New Delhi, India
e-mail: raju@rrchandran.com; raju.r532@gmail.com

T. S. Sridhar
St. John's Research Institute, Bengaluru, India
e-mail: tssridhar@sjri.res.in

S. Iyengar
Dharampur, India
e-mail: sudarshan54@gmail.com

S. Vidyasagar and P. Hatti (eds.), *Leadership and Role Modelling*,
Palgrave Studies in Leadership and Followership,
https://doi.org/10.1007/978-3-319-69056-8_8

someone I have admired since the beginning of my law practice nearly 41 years ago.

In the course of these long years, I have had many models in the profession. Apart from Andhyarujina, I have looked up to Soli Sorabjee, Fali Nariman, the late S. V. Gupte, B. Sen, and my own senior, the late M. K. Ramamurthi. And a contemporary just four years older than me: the late Vinod Bobde. This is of course, not an exhaustive list. High professional integrity is common to all my heroes, living or dead. Fairness and detachment are their other professional qualities which I have admired.

I have had role models not only in the legal profession but in the field of journalism as well. For writing readable prose, I have admired lawyer-commentator A. G. Noorani and the late journalists of yesteryear, Frank Moraes, Sham Lal, Inder Malhotra, and B. G. Verghese.

Have all my role models been positive, or have there been negative role models as well? I wonder if the concept of a standalone 'negative' role model exists. Like all humans, every role model of mine has had flaws. And so, when I have resolved to emulate one or the other in aspects which I have admired, I have also told myself to avoid the mistakes which they have made and to do some things very differently from how they did them. After all, no one wants to be a mere clone!

It is inevitable that one has had different role models at different stages of one's life and career, and so one does 'outgrow' a role model at times. But this is never a reflection on them. And when a role model has disappointed me, there has never been a forsaking of a relationship, because I have been as understanding and forgiving of them as I am of myself and as I would expect others to be of me. I have also felt sobered by the thought that I might have disappointed my role models, and also that I might be disappointing those for whom I might be a role model.

Some of my role models were persons with whom I was in close contact, while others were persons I admired from a distance. But ultimately, in the course of these long years of practice, I have been able to meet all my distant heroes as well, and I have been able to tell them that they have influenced me. Modesty is a quality I admire, and none of my models have let me down on that score: they have all been self-deprecating, when I have expressed my admiration for them. Role models with whom I have been in close touch have given freely of their time to me, whenever I have needed their advice or even when I have just needed a sounding board. My interactions with them have made me feel comfortable about being my own person, in a profession where there are some set notions of achievement and success.

The practice of law confronts one with dilemmas every other day and one never has all the answers. There are dilemmas about how best to handle difficult cases and also how to handle difficult judges in not-so-difficult cases. There are dilemmas about how to tell a judge that his/her conduct is not fair or that he/she might have a conflict of interest. There are possibilities of conflict of interest in briefs which come to you, some direct conflicts which are not difficult to take a decision about but some indirect conflicts where you need wise counsel. In such situations, I have turned to my role models.

Choosing a role model has never been a conscious or cognitive process for me. It has always been a matter of chemistry. There's a certain kind of chemistry with those I have seen closely in flesh and blood, and an equally potent chemistry which has worked long distance with others. What exactly do I mean by 'chemistry'? There are some qualities and attributes which make me click with someone else. Such as courtesy, humility, meticulousness in language, a crazy sense of humour, punctuality, their taste in literature and music, their dressing sense. This, of course, does not mean that I am only comfortable with people similar to me. People very different to me have also been role models because you learn more from those who live their lives differently from you. It makes you less smug about yourself.

At this stage of my life, there are naturally fewer role models, because many have died. But since there is no retirement age in my profession, there are still some professional elders around to whom I look up. But while I am on the subject of retirement, I must confess that I hope to retire some day. And that's where I am facing a dearth of role models. Not many have retired at a stage where people have asked 'Why?' instead of the unpleasant 'Why not?'. We expect our sportsmen to listen to their bodies; should we lawyers also not listen to our bodies and minds?

It would, of course, be presumptuous and immodest to see myself as a role model. But the 'guru–*shishya*' tradition which the legal profession follows pitchforks you into that position. Your style of advocacy, your interactions with instructing lawyers and clients, and the way you conduct yourself with your staff are all matters of close observation by junior colleagues, and you are always conscious of the example you are setting.

With the legal profession today being much larger than it used to be, there is difficulty in finding quality mentors. A large number of young people join the profession but there aren't enough 'seniors' to take in every junior who comes in. And a senior cannot be expected to take on every junior who applies, irrespective of merit and aptitude. So, many may have to adopt distant role models who won't be mentoring them. Unfortunately, it is not possible at all to formalise role modelling for individual legal practitioners and to impose any code on them to ensure diversity. Taking on a junior lawyer in an individual practitioner's chamber again needs the right chemistry between 'the guru' and 'the *shishya*'. Also, in a public service-oriented profession such as law, where every conscientious lawyer endeavours to give the best legal service to the client, the merit of an entrant to a chamber is important. In the name of diversity, no professional would want the professional reputation of the chamber to suffer. Having said that, there is definitely a need to sensitise 'Seniors' to try and maintain diversity in their recruitments. This is particularly necessary in a hereditary and dynastic profession such as the legal profession where bright young lawyers who don't have 'legal' pedigree feel that they are at a disadvantage compared to those with a legal background in the matter of recruitment. So, while talking of diversity in the legal profession we should not only think of gender, caste, and region but also of those who don't have legal blood in their veins.

Judges also need role models in the difficult art of judging. Subconsciously, every lawyer who becomes a judge would follow the judges whom he/she has admired while appearing as a lawyer. Just as a lawyer, based on his own temperament, would be drawn to an aggressive or a gentlemanly lawyer, a new judge could either be drawn to a quick and impatient 'problem-solving' judge or to a laidback, scholarly judge. But for both judges and lawyers, it is important to have a diverse set of models in terms of gender, social background, and so on, to make them sensitive, humane, and compassionate in their work.

With those who see their own professions as the best in the world and for whom their work is their life, there is little likelihood of having role models outside their profession. But for those who see their professions in a larger social context, and as one of many equally important ones, there might be role models outside their professions. The ethics of other professions, the approach of other professionals to their work and their way of balancing work and life might offer lessons to those who are willing to learn.

The Personae of Role Models in Medicine and Research

T. S. Sridhar

Having had the privilege of being in formal training for an inordinately long period in two very different domains—clinical medicine and experimental biological research—I have been the beneficiary of having had a wide range of role models whose behaviours have had a deep impact on my professional and personal development.

While it is almost implicitly assumed that the primary method of learning medicine is by osmosis from colleagues and preceptors, role models are central to the inculcation of clinical skills. Historically, the method of acquiring the knowledge and skills of medical practice was by the process of apprenticeship. Such a process included some didactic learning but comprised mostly of on-the-job learning. Although the current organisation of medical colleges and teaching hospitals for large classes of students seems to have moved away from the traditional model, it, in fact, preserves the core of the apprenticeship model, in particular, during the internship and post-graduation phases.

Coming from a culture in which iconography is pervasive and having studied at a time (the 1980s) when the organisation of professional learning was very paternalistic, I have been deeply influenced by multiple role models. Having studied and worked in both India and the United States, my experience of role modelling has been that the national ethnocultural context (India versus the United States) seems to matter less, and the individual (model and follower) matters more. However, as I mention later, when it came to mentoring, the nature of this was distinctly different in the domains of clinical medicine and scientific experimental research.

In medicine, for the most part, my role models were senior professors and clinicians whose skills of diagnosis, surgery, and clinical management left us students in awe. A charismatic individual holds a particular sway on the minds of impressionable juniors, and the role model is seen to be the 'redeemer' working against larger-than-life forces. The choice of a particular individual amongst the many most likely reflects personal inclinations and sensitivities. For example, as an individual brought up on a healthy dose of Sherlock Holmes' exploits, I leaned towards physicians with extraordinary diagnostic skills as role models, whereas a surgically inclined person would be more likely to pick an individual with superior motor skills. If I were to reflect further on my choices, I would also have to say that background was not necessarily a consideration, nor was gender (not least because I worked at a time when, unfortunately, the majority of our senior professors were male), although, this might reflect both a lack of proximity as well as sensitivity to these matters. In almost all instances, however, the 'person' was hidden behind the persona, and hidden within this selection of role models is a significant element of hero worship.

Medicine has a tradition of creating myths and legends around characters, many of whom are admirable but quite often intimidating as well. The childish desire to acquire these quasi-magical capabilities is almost a rite of passage in medicine. With time, obviously, some of the abilities appear more pedestrian especially as one masters these skills, but the awe inspired by particularly complex attributes endure. To elaborate, the learning of the ethical dimensions of medical practice, especially compassion, was almost entirely by the use of particular doctors as role models. And not just compassion, a host of other qualities are probably best learnt by observation. The first being observation itself. In addition, decision-making in emergencies, dealing with anxious relatives, the way one treats the ancillary medical staff, in particular, nurses and aides who are the life-blood of a hospital system, are best learnt by emulating the behaviour of the very best. It is perhaps here that I should add that in modelling interactions with the rest of the team, negative role models abound, both in the operating theatre and the hospital ward. While there is a lot of hand-wringing today about the lack of high-minded individuals in the current practice of medicine, I am convinced that there cannot be too many methods that have a higher impact.

My experiences of role models in my research training were as intense, with some important differences. There is a fundamental divide between the cultures of scientific research and the practice of clinical medicine in a busy hospital. Out of necessity, the hospital command structure is arranged in a hierarchical manner, not least because of the doctrine of vicarious responsibility of the consultant doctor. An ideal research environment, on the other hand, encourages scepticism as well as an informality of interaction between the supervisor and student, since both are subservient to the 'truth', whatever that is construed to be in science. Hence, it is possible in a research setting to arrive at the choice of one's role model without the influence of power that inevitably influences young minds.

Given these circumstances, quite often, my role models during research training were not always the people in our teaching faculty. The sciences in the twentieth century have had literally hundreds of virtuoso practitioners whose exploits have received wide publicity, at least within the scientific world. For example, Albert Einstein was, has been, and continues to be an inspirational role model. However, for me he is an inspiration not only for his universally acknowledged accomplishments but also more for his philosophical attitude towards trying to comprehend the unknown, which is very humbling. Other role models were faculty whose cognitive skills, especially the honed analytical abilities, created in us the desire to emulate them.

During the times in which I trained, especially the 1980s, many of the best role models were just being their natural selves and if there was the awareness in them that they were being scrutinised intensely, they seemed unaware of it. However, a conspicuous difference between then and now was the lack of serious mentoring by my Indian role models.

It was only during my training in the United States in the 1990s that I came across the type of serious time-intensive mentoring that is now assumed to be part of the responsibility of a research faculty.

As can be seen, almost all my role models in both the training in clinical medicine as well as in experimental research were almost entirely positive. This is not to deny the presence of base individuals in both medicine as well as research, but I would not use the term ‘role model’ in describing them, for the connotation of the word is almost entirely positive.

I have spent the last 10 years as a faculty member in a medical research organisation where one of my principal responsibilities is to help young researchers develop the skills necessary to apply the methods of research to the solution of critical problems in medicine. In this role, I have had to be both role model as well as mentor. To me, being a role model has been mostly trying to do the right thing as far as possible. Sometimes this does need deliberation, and if it doesn’t sound trite, it means to largely hold one’s behaviour to high ideals. Being a mentor is entirely different, however, for it is taking the time to understand the situation, desires, and capabilities of the mentee. This is a time-consuming interactive process that demands sensitivity and acceptance of individual differences, while encouraging the growth of the mentee over a long period of time, usually lasting many years.

There are newer dimensions and challenges in being a role model and mentor today. There is now both the acknowledgement and recognition of unethical approaches to research ranging from plagiarism to falsification of results to the blatant usurping of credit. Being in a position of responsibility as a doctoral or postdoctoral supervisor places significant demands on our willingness to discuss these matters in a fair and transparent manner and lay the boundaries of acceptable behaviour to the trainees. I guess I am an old-fashioned chap, for I do believe that in the ultimate analysis it is by holding oneself to the highest ideals and by being true to oneself that one can hope to be a role model for the people being trained by us.

Role Modelling as an Exercise in Self-Reflection

Sudarshan Iyengar

I have worked in distinctively different types of institutions, as a teacher, researcher, and administrator. I did not consciously realise that I had chosen some persons as my role models during this time, although *in life*, I have followed a distant person as my role model. The invitation to write about workplace role models has prompted me to reflect on this. I have understood that in Indian culture, until recent times, the idea of a role model was perceived to be the *aadarsha purusha* (ideal man)—to be followed by men, and *aadarsha stree* (ideal woman)—to be followed by women. Human existence went beyond body alone and hence one's behaviour and action had to be oriented towards the growth of the soul that lived in the body. I don't claim to be spiritual, but I have chosen Mahatma Gandhi, for whom the ultimate goal was *moksha* (salvation), as my distant role model. His quest was the Truth, being truthful was his act, and his role model was *Satyavadi Raja* Harishchandra (the truthful king Harishchandra).

My professional career began in a college, as a lecturer teaching undergraduate courses. My role model, in an unconscious way, was a teacher from my university days. He was not an outstanding scholar with fame. But he was a wonderful teacher. As a student, I was impressed that a teacher should teach the subject the way he did. I enjoyed his classes. Learning economics with the story that went behind the development of thought and theory was a very interesting way of learning and teaching. For instance, he would tell the class about the economist, his profession, and the circumstances in which he or she had worked on a theory. His language was simple, diction clear, and delivery was at a pace that even the not-so-bright students could follow him. He would try to take the entire class with him. Later I learnt that a role model in any walk of life becomes one because he or she tries successfully to carry the team. He was successful in demonstrating proper behaviour and action for the profession. I have since made it a practice to teach and conduct academic sessions by weaving in human stories with theory and thought. I have received good responses.

I have spent a long time working in social sciences research institutes. One must be good and professional in conducting and reporting research. As I entered the field, I found many researchers and academicians who were doing excellently. However, most of them were distant. But I had two role models who helped me. They had published significantly in peer-reviewed publications and contributed effectively to policy formulation in the country. One of them is also an accomplished teacher in a high-ranked management institute. Both were largely positive role models, but with a shade of negativity. They were my supervisors and guides and I interacted with them regularly. In that sense, both have been my mentors as well. I did not necessarily emulate them in everything, but both of them were excellent leaders and role models for many others.

Conducting field research on economic aspects is a tough task. My first role model was a senior in college and had impressed me even during the university days. He had begun publishing research papers as a graduate student. He was a natural leader in academics. Clarity of thought, intelligence, and hard work were his qualities. He could provide a way to train fellow students and juniors and at times seniors too, and improve their research capabilities. Later in his professional career, when I assisted him during research in a field situation on decentralised planning exercises, I realised that he had an effect on both the individual researcher and those who were part of a larger team.

I met and worked with my second role model at the workplace, when I had already established myself as a good researcher and promising academic. He was intelligent and a person with clarity of thought. He was honest and blunt in giving opinions. He was also caring but lacked expression. He was the director of the institute where I worked. He groomed me for it, but I was not aware of it. Only when I became the director of the institute myself did I realise that he had prepared me to take on the responsibility later. In his career, he has led many research surveys and trained dozens of researchers in field surveys. When I joined a university, and became its vice chancellor, I was able to become a leader and role model for the faculty in conducting field research and reporting.

Conducting social science research calls for exacting preparation. Most of the inquiry involves exploring situations through data collection, analysis, and interpretation. In this exercise, constructing inquiry instruments and preparing most relevant checklists are critical requirements. Both my role models insisted on sound preparatory work. Their intelligence, sharpness, diligence, and skill in preparing research instruments were highly impressive. I tried sincerely to cultivate at least the diligence and the skill; the former two qualities were given to me and I could improve marginally. My second role model excelled in conducting surveys and he had reached the top echelons of the national survey body known as National Sample Survey Organisation (NSSO). He was also advisor to, and headed, various committees constituted by the Registrar General of Census Operations of the Indian government.

Reporting research is a crucial part of the work. Both my role models were very good at it. I lacked both the language and the content. The shade of negativity I mentioned relates to the arrogance with which they supervised my work. I was keenly aware of my serious limitations and hence yielded to the way they guided me to improve. One of them would simply throw the first draft that I prepared into the dustbin and asked me to write again! This could be very jarring at times and hurtful because the effort to prepare the 'useless draft' was also immense. But what I admired in them and wanted to emulate was the clarity with which they could do it. I did feel hurt, but I came around as I knew that I had not done a good job, even with all effort that I had put in. The other solace was that they always assured that I had data—qualitative and quantitative—but had failed to report it appropriately. My second role model wrote with clarity and brevity. He would not 'pass' any draft without reading it line by line. This led to delays, sometimes inordinate, but he would clear every word before it went public. He would say, 'Sudarshan, once you publish, the reader cannot enter your head and understand what you want to say, so please say it in your writing!' The negativity this entailed was the belief that his was the only way of doing things! I believed that it was not, and did not want to be like him in that regard.

When I look at both these individuals as role models and leaders in the workplace, I find that they could be and were mentors. They demonstrated confidence and leadership by being calm and confident. Knowledgeable and fearlessly unique, they usually showed respect and concern for others. They communicated reasonably well with most people. With these characteristics, they were mostly able to make the team work and get positive outcomes.

Do I want to be a role model in workplace? Yes and no. Yes, because the organisation in which one works has goals and objectives. The work processes are mostly laid out clearly, although there is always scope for improvement. One's own behaviour and conduct should convince colleagues, co-workers, and followers that the person guiding them is honest and sincere in following what one says and does. The most important point is that one must do what one says and expect others to do the same—therein lies honesty. Leading by example is the key. It should never be a put-on show. Sincerity lies in making an all-out effort towards agreed goals, objectives, and targets.

No, because I have been a person who is evolving, trying to meet the expectations that have been set for me, as well as the expectations I have set for myself. The honesty and sincerity needed in 'walking the talk' are not, I believe, of the grade that would pass for being (or becoming) a role model.

Nevertheless, it is likely that others follow one as a role model without declaring it. Presumably, I have been a leader and role model in the various institutions in which I have worked and led. I have received feedback after completing my term in each organisation. I don't think I have been adjudged fearlessly unique, but I have been recognised as knowledgeable and well rounded. The latter quality has made me humble, a person who respects one and all and shows concern for all, irrespective of the status of the person. I have been told that I interact and communicate with everyone and no one feels alienated. I am easily approachable. I am confident and take decisions and carry most of the team with me. These outcomes have been positive, and some colleagues have followed me as a leader and role model.

Finally, I focus on my life's role model, Gandhiji. I stated in the beginning that in the context of Indian cultural ethos and philosophical foundations my role model is Gandhiji. This now needs some elaboration. Gandhiji said 'my life is my message'. He considered himself a *mumukshu* (a person on a spiritual pursuit). However, 'this-world'ly affairs were very important to him and his earnest desire was to use his bodily existence in the service of humanity. His quest, pursuit, and social concern, are all beautifully expressed in the Introduction to his autobiography. He says:

> I simply want to tell the story of my numerous experiments with truth, and as my life consists of nothing but those experiments.... My experiments in the political field are now known, not only in India, but to a certain extent to the 'civilized' world.... If the experiments are really spiritual, then there can be no room for self-praise....
>
> What I want to achieve—what I have been striving and pining to achieve these thirty years—is self-realization, to see God face to face, to attain *moksha*. I live and move and have my being in pursuit of this goal. All that I do by way of speaking and writing, and all my ventures in the political field, are directed to this same end. But as I have all along believed that what is possible for one is possible for all, my experiments have not been conducted in the closet, but in the open; and I do not think that this fact detracts from their spiritual value....
>
> I hope and pray that no one will regard the advice interspersed in the following chapters as authoritative. The experiments narrated should be regarded as illustrations, in the light of which everyone may carry on his own experiments according to his own inclinations and capacity.

(Gandhi, 2006, pp. ix–xii)

In accepting Gandhiji as a role model, one must commit to 'walk the talk'. The distance between what one says and what one does must be minimal. In fact, in this process, there is no conscious effort to follow a role model. The development of oneself as a professional and as an individual no longer remains dichotomous. The aim of an individual in life is to grow fully within, and as a consequence, without. The without can be professional and a leading professional. There is no divergence between private space and public space (working space). In a postmodernist analytical discourse Lloyd and Susan Rudolph (Rudolph & Rudolph, 2006) discuss this issue very well. They say that in every country in modern times people have, in some way, begun worrying about the private morality of their leaders. Some continuity is found between a man's personal self-indulgence or self-restraint and his capacity to act disinterestedly in the matter of state and general welfare. The same applies to leaders in other sectors, including business. In the West, it has come to be assumed that the process of differentiation that characterises our lives, and which touches all our affairs, has made private morals less relevant for public action. They go on to argue to that certain constitutional assumptions also lie behind the belief that private behaviour is, to a point, irrelevant to public, in a public man. Gandhiji, however, said that he derived from his experiments in the spiritual realm the powers he exercised in the political field, and Lloyd and Susan Rudolph accept this as the better position. He firmly believed that private morality had public consequences, and hence, ethical restraints practised by the self are better than institutional restraints.

In accepting Gandhiji as a role model an important shift of values takes place within the individual liberty discourse. In the Western discourse, the value of competition is established, while in Gandhi's discourse, which admittedly draws from the Indian philosophical discourse, the value of cooperation is established. No one is in competition. Each must pursue salvation in his or her own unique way. For material survival, cooperation has better potential to give harmonious results. A person must be eternally vigilant so that no divergence occurs. Eternal vigilance involves three aspects in dealing with the inner self: *aatma nirikshan*, *aatma parikshan*, and *aatma shodhan*—self-reflection, self-examination, and self-correction, respectively. In a peculiar way then, each individual is her or his own role model!

References

Gandhi, M. K. (2006). *An autobiography* (*The story of my experiments with truth*) (M. Desai, Trans.). Ahmedabad, India: Navajivan Publishing Trust.

Rudolph, L. I., & Rudolph, S. H. (2006). Self-control and political potency. In L. I. Rudolph & S. H. Rudolph (Eds.), *Postmodern Gandhi and other essays: Gandhi in the world and at home* (pp. 207–229). New Delhi: Oxford University Press.

Index

S. Vidyasagar and P. Hatti (eds.), *Leadership and Role Modelling*,
Palgrave Studies in Leadership and Followership,
https://doi.org/10.1007/978-3-319-69056-8

Kolibri 360 GmbH
Ferdinand-Jühlke-Straße 7
99095 Erfurt, Deutschland
produktsicherheit@kolibri360.de